Behind the Collar

A Pastor's Wife's Journey From Illusion to Reality

Sheila K. Dasch

BȾC

"I am the vine; you are the branches. If you remain in in me and I in you, you will bear much fruit; apart from me you can do nothing.

John 15.5

Acknowledgments

I thank God in my prayers every day. Today, I would also like to publicly thank Him for His grace and presence in my life. He is the one who brought me from where I was to where I am today, Behind the Collar. To God be the glory!

To my biological family, thank you for your continued love and support. A special thanks to my mom, who always made sure we were in church on Sundays, where my faith journey began. I am thankful for my church family, St. Mark in Houston, and my church family St. John, in Mansfield. My life is richer because of you. You have blessed me with mentoring, kindness, and encouragement along this journey. I will forever call you "my family."

I am truly grateful for my circles and circles of WOW friends. Thank you for your support, love, and acceptance. I am blessed by you! You know who you are!

A big thanks to the Lucio family for posing for the cover of my book. Thank you, Richard, for the handsome neck and chin shot. Thank you, Bella, for those gorgeous hands supporting the collar. Thank you, Leah, for taking the picture! I appreciate you all!

I would also like to thank my husband, who was the collar behind this journey. You have been the rock and role model for our family, and I thank God for you. We have had an amazing journey with peaks and valleys. I can't imagine being on this ride with anyone else. Thank you for encouraging me to write my story even though it was one-sided… mine. lol

To my editor, Kathleen Seger, thank you for your time, energy and words that helped make this book special.

Finally, to all the pastors' wives I have met on this journey, thank you for being you as I learned to be me.

Table Of Contents

Chapter 1

I Thought He
Walked on Water

*O*h no—he can't be a pastor! What is he doing in a bar dancing and drinking beer?

It was a country and western bar in a small college town where people gathered to have fun on a Friday night. My girlfriends and I had gone there to meet friends and dance. He and his friend had walked up to our table and asked us to dance. He wore jeans, a fitted pullover shirt showing off his nice physique, and had a devilish smile. He wasn't that great of a dancer, otherwise—he was the man I'd fantasized about meeting. What a fun night! We danced, drank beer, and got to know each other. Later, my friend whispered to me, "He is a pastor."

Oh no, tell me it ain't so!

I grew up going to a Southern Baptist Church, and I believed pastors were close to perfect. Next to Moses and Jesus was my pastor. Pastors knew the bible and preached against sin. They were as close to God as anyone could get. I never expected to meet a pastor in a bar, much less one who was drinking beer and dancing. I didn't know what to think! Then he asked me to have lunch with him that following Monday, and how do you think I responded? Hmmmmm... I said, "YES!"

Our first date was lunch at a nice restaurant in my hometown. I wasn't sure how this would go. What should I wear? I was going to lunch with someone I just met, was attracted to, and he was a pastor. What would he wear? What did he drive? How should I act?

He pulled into the driveway where I lived in a black Oldsmobile Cutlass, a fairly conservative car for that day. Again, he was dressed in jeans and a fitted pullover shirt. I guess I wasn't expecting a pastor to look so hot! I wore a nice sundress, and I could tell it caught his eye. He was such a gentleman, making sure he opened the car door for me to get in and to get out. We went to a steakhouse for lunch. I was a little nervous, thinking I should act differently than I usually did on a date. I had no problem talking with him when I thought he was just one of the guys, but what do I say to a pastor? Do I talk about Genesis, Exodus, Leviticus, Numbers, Deuteronomy? Would he ask me to recite the ten commandments? What was I going to talk to him about? I was nervous! Although I wasn't that hungry, I was so anxious that I cut into my steak the moment it arrived. As I opened my mouth to take a bite, he cleared his throat and asked, "Do you mind if we pray first?" I was embarrassed! What have I done? I thought, I must be a heathen… what if he really does ask me to recite the ten commandments? I wasn't sure I could. The only one I could think of was, "Thou shall not mess with a pastor!" I assumed he must walk on water.

Speaking of water, after lunch, he asked me, "Would you like to drive out by the lake?" He had said he loved to fish. I assumed he wanted to see how the fishing was. As I would soon find out, he was more interested in me than the fish. We drove around and checked out some of the fishing spots. He then parked his car under a big oak tree. As we both got out of the car, he reached into the backseat and pulled out a silver bucket with a chilled bottle of champagne and two fluted glasses. Popping the cork, he poured the champagne, and we toasted meeting each other. I never expected to be romanced by a pastor. To my surprise, he was turning out to be a "romantic devil."

Later, he brought me back to my house. Then the handsome pastor kissed me goodbye at the front door. How romantic! I think I fell head over heels for him on that first date. Authors Jackson and Leder in their book Mirages of Marriage state that many couples describe their feelings at the beginning of their relationship as "ecstatic."[i]

That may be true since ecstatic comes from the Greek word "ecstasis" which means "deranged or beside oneself." That was me, and perhaps you when you first started dating your spouse. Where did my common sense go? I was dating not just a man, I was dating a pastor! We went on to date for four years before he popped the question. Today, we have been married 34 years. My husband, who thinks he is funny, tells people we have been happily married 30 years. Then he says, "We just celebrated our 34th anniversary." There may be some truth to that!

During the course of our courtship, I discovered that my husband was a bit more human than I thought. From kissing me on the front porch after that first date to waterskiing, he seemed like everyone else. I have seen him at his best and at his worst. I have learned that, despite my initial thoughts, he does not walk on water. He sinks! He needs Jesus just like I do. Just like we all do.

I had no idea what married life with a pastor would be like. I never thought, I am marrying a Pastor. I thought I was just marrying a man. Maybe I didn't say that quite right. I married a man who was a pastor, not a pastor who was a man. At first, I was a little surprised by how people perceived my role. I was almost always introduced as the pastor's wife. I sometimes thought that was my name. And for a long time, I did not understand what people expected of me in this role.

I don't know if you've ever considered what it would be like to live with a man who works for God. Here is what I pondered when I got married and became a "pastor's wife." Would I always be in church every Sunday, every Wednesday, every baptism, every wedding, every event? Would I have to wear long dresses? (I had some cute short ones.) Would people expect me to sing in the choir? Lead women's bible studies? Teach Sunday school? I began to wonder if I could live Behind the Collar. What I learned from this journey, from all these questions and expectations after 34 years of marriage to a man who is a pastor, is what I will share with you in this book.

This is the story of my journey from illusion to reality, from insecurity to significance, and from religion to relationship! It may not be comfortable to read. It was, at times, not comfortable to live. There were peaks and valleys, sorrows and blessings. I came out on the other side of my journey feeling blessed. But I was not there at the beginning. Even now, I am still learning what it means to live joyfully Behind the Collar. It is a journey that will last the rest of my life.

The Apostle Paul said, "I have learned to be content whatever the circumstances." (Philippians 4.11) When he wrote those words, Paul was a prisoner behind bars, looking from the inside out. I am a woman married to a man who is still a pastor. I still live Behind the Collar, but I have learned to live not under the circumstances but above them. It's a learning curve. As Paul said, "I have learned." I want to help you shorten your learning curve and encourage you so you can face your circumstances and live above them by God's love and power.

You will discover that even through the messes of my journey, God used the mess to bring a message of hope, joy, forgiveness, and strength. My prayer is that my story may encourage women who live Behind the Collar. Perhaps this journey will also help churches as they minister to pastors' wives. This book will also help pastors come to a realization of the reality of the stressors and expectations put on their wife. Everyone who reads this book will gain a better understanding of the person and the role of what we call the pastors' wife. Everything can end well... trust me!

Now, turn the page and discover the Journey from Illusion to Reality—Behind the Collar.

Chapter 2

Lonely Days and
Lonely Nights

The loneliness Behind the Collar shocked me. I didn't expect it at all. I was young and in love and excited to move from my small town of 20,000 people to the big city of Houston, population 3 million. I was well known in my small town, but when I moved to Houston, no one knew me. I was a stranger.

My husband was the Pastor of Singles and Counseling at a large church in Houston. It was in the top 1% of churches in America in attendance. He had been serving there for three years prior to our marriage. While he was established and had many friends, I knew only him. I had met some people in the church during our courtship but had not made any friends yet.

Because of this, I wanted to be with my new husband constantly. We were newlyweds, and he was my security blanket. Everything, exciting as it was, was new to me! I felt like I was living on another planet. Amid all this change, my lack of connections made me unsure of myself. It did not help that he led a large singles group and needed to be at singles events. I learned quickly that I was not going to fit in like I had all my life. The ladies of the group were not as excited about my marriage as I was. For some, my husband had been a vital part of their social life. For others, he was the secret object of their affection. Can you see where this was going? I felt like an outsider. I did not belong! I began to experience loneliness—big time.

I once read that loneliness is a state of mind. The state I was in was Texas, and I felt Texas sized loneliness. I was surrounded by millions of people, yet I didn't feel connected. Instead, I felt sad, empty, and cut off from others. I had no social support from friends, family, or peers. I had moved from the familiar to the unfamiliar and felt lost. This loneliness was killing my optimism.

A study of pastors' wives found that, "The number one challenge for pastors' wives is loneliness."[ii] Overwhelmingly, pastors' wives reported loneliness as the biggest challenge they faced, and continue to face. Many of these ladies had no true confidants. Some had scars from past relationships. More than a few had experienced depression. Some still do. If I had been asked what the biggest challenge Behind the Collar was for me, my response would have been the same as the others—loneliness. I felt a deep isolation.

In this less than welcoming new life, I blindly smiled and thought, "At least I've got my husband." Genesis 2.18 says, "It is not good for the man to be alone." Well, it was not good for a woman to be alone either. In my isolation, I began to have doubts about myself and my husband.

When I married my husband, I thought pastors worked mostly on Sundays, and maybe a few hours during the week. I never fathomed that many worked 50 to 60 hours a week. I know what you're thinking, "How did you date him for four years without knowing that?" Our courtship was a long distance one. We lived five hours apart, so we wrote letters weekly. When I was able to go to Houston or he was able to visit me, we focused on each other, not work.

I was deep in the illusion that we would be together nearly all of the time. The reality check I cashed told me differently. He served in a ministry he loved that included a singles group and lots of events. I just couldn't believe he would leave in the morning for work and not come home sometimes until 9:00 or 10:00 p.m. I began to have doubts and suspicions. What if he was meeting with another woman? Crazy thoughts ran through my head.

Let me tell you how crazy I got! On more than a few occasions, we would finish breakfast and he would leave to go to work. I would still be in my PJs. As soon as he pulled out of the driveway, I would jump in my car and follow him to see where he was going. I was certain he was not going to work. We lived about 20 minutes away from the church, so I would follow him at a distance. I followed him, guess where? Straight to church! Every time! I wasted a lot of gasoline that year. It wasn't another woman devouring his time, it was the church. In *Charisma Leader Magazine*, a pastor's wife said, "Frankly, the church is like a mistress to my husband. He has abandoned me for someone else."[iii] My husband had not completely abandoned me, but if I was on a diet, this would be pretty slim rations. I didn't like the taste of it either. The philosopher, Kahlil Gibran said, "Let there be spaces in your togetherness."[iv] My relationship with my husband had plenty of empty spaces.

This was the reality of my life Behind the Collar during the first year of my marriage. I had not yet built the kind of relationships where I could talk, confide in, and be real. Those kinds of relationships don't just happen. My husband was my only confidante, and I could not admit to him that I was having doubts every time he walked out the door. On the outside, I remained strong, but on the inside, I was screaming.

I did some crazy things that first year of marriage because no one had prepared me for being a pastor's wife. I was newly married. I had moved to a large city where I didn't know anyone. I had just graduated from college but decided to put my career on hold while I adjusted to this new life.

It took me two years to begin to come to terms with my new reality. I finally decided not to wait on other people, but to reach out to them. Looking back, I had begun to see myself as a victim. But I was not going to play that role anymore. I took responsibility for making friends and dealing with my loneliness. Now, I am not saying all you need to do to deal with loneliness is to have a lot of friends. I am saying I realized I could sit back and moan and groan, or I could reach out and take a chance by meeting new people. After all, this was my new life. I said goodbye to the old idea that everyone was going to naturally embrace me. The reality was—I needed to embrace others first.

My Birkman Profile (a personality inventory) revealed that I was a very social person. I learned that I needed, not wanted, *needed* to be around people. It even showed that I recharged when I was tired by being around people. What it didn't say was that I needed to be around some people I could be "real" with. I needed to be around people who saw me as a person, not only the pastor's wife. I needed a close friend.

For most pastors' wives, loneliness is our greatest challenge. We are often unsure who we can trust to keep things confidential. We keep things private. We put on a mask that hides our loneliness and have loose connections.

How did I handle my loneliness? Once I quit singing "Lonely Days and Lonely Nights," this is how I took responsibility for my feelings. I reached out to others and discovered who could potentially be a good friend. I decided to meet with small groups of people in this big city and bring to my life and theirs, a little bit of country.

I also started making our church my little bit of country. I settled into this big city by making it smaller. I built connections. The outsider (me) became an insider. I began to feel like I belonged.

How did I make connections? This may not be a prescription for you, but it worked for me. I volunteered in the church office. I also helped my husband by typing his doctoral dissertation through revision after revision... and we still remained married! Amazing Grace!

I am not much of a singer, but I love to sing! I joined our young contemporary choir and made some good friends and connections. My loneliness began to fade as I reached out and got involved. I couldn't play the piano, but I could play softball. So I joined the ladies' softball team. There is a story that still is told around Houston about the first time I got up to bat. I was a thin girl (*emphasis on was*), and the coach motioned for everyone to move in a little closer. To everyone's surprise, on the first pitch, I hit the ball over their heads, out of our ball field, and across the next ball field! It was a home run! That might have been the moment I was accepted by that group. I made some great home-run friends there.

I remember being asked if I would teach Sunday School. I didn't feel like I was theologically prepared to teach the Bible, but I did teach aerobics. So, I started an exercise class at our church. We were called the Firm Believers. We filled the gym with 50 to 60 people, men and women ranging from high schoolers to one man in his 70's. We had people from outside the church attend class as well.

It did not take long to get to know people and make friends at this large church. As they say today, "These are my tribe." Your tribe are the ones to whom you can tell your mistakes and fears. They will be with you forever. I have learned that to make a friend, you need to be a friend. If you are feeling lonely, and we all do at times, figure out what you need to do to deal with your loneliness and do it.

Today, I still have close friends in Houston. Even though I live five hours away I remain in contact with them. I know I can count on them and they can count on me.

There are many routes you can take to deal with loneliness during your journey. What I did may or may not be useful to you. Sometimes, people need more than just a friend. A professional counselor is a good listener and can help you deal with some issues. And get this—they don't tell anyone else.

Perhaps you are reading this and thinking, "Yeah, but you don't understand my situation." You may be right. But I want you to know that there is someone out there who understands you completely. Perhaps He understands you better than you think. He is your

Father in Heaven, and He is a good Father. He is for you, not against you.

He created the church. Jesus died for it and for you. The church is the body of Christ on this planet. There are people God has put in your path to travel alongside you. You were created for relationships. Reach out. What have you got to lose—your pride? What have you got to gain—a friend.

Jesus said to His disciples, "I no longer call you my servants, I have called you friends" (John 15.15). He knows that you need friends. He even knows that sometimes friends betray you. But He will never betray you. He loves you and gives your life meaning.

My journey led me to people, but first, God led me to Him. In His word, He told me who I am—a child of God. His word told me that I was not an accident, that I was one of a kind. I discovered that I could have been born at any time in history, but God had me born for such a time as this. I discovered that God gave me talents and gifts. All this applies to you as well. Nobody else on this planet has your fingerprints. You are unique. The earth sits at 23 degrees on its axis. Any other angle, and life as we know it would not exist on this planet. You and I were both put here intentionally. Everything that I discovered was true for me, but it's also true for YOU. You are a gifted child of God. What would happen if you started taking steps to deal with your loneliness? What if you called someone tonight?

Perhaps you would discover renewed energy and joy Behind the Collar.

Chapter 3

Everybody Needs Somebody

Everybody needs somebody. John Donne wrote, "No man is an island."[v] He could have just as easily said, "No pastor's wife is an island." Lifeway research on pastors' wives painted a troublesome picture of them and close connections. They found that only one out of ten said they can count on friends in the church a great deal when they are under stress.[vi] The reality is there are a lot of islands, a lot of disconnected pastors' wives out there in America.

After the first two years of living Behind the Collar, I started getting better at my role. I decided that I wanted to accelerate my growth in a positive way. I thought, "If I'm going to be a pastor's wife, I want to be the best one I can be." I had a lofty view of pastors' wives. I looked up to them. I wanted to be like them. So, I did what everyone does. I looked for a shortcut to maturity. I wanted to leap into the future and become the "perfect pastor's wife."

Wouldn't you know it? God gave me what I had been praying for. A letter arrived in the mail inviting me to attend a retreat for pastor's wives at Camp Lone Star in La Grange, Texas. I jumped for joy when I read the letter. This must be God sent! I imagined myself at the retreat with a bunch of women who were married to pastors and talking to these women who were seasoned in their role. If I could learn from them, I could move ahead at the speed of light (I'm a quick learner). All I had to do was attend the retreat. Then I would be like them.

In the church where my husband pastored, there were three pastors' wives. One of them decided that she would also like to attend the retreat. We got together and made plans to drive the 100 miles to the retreat and mingle, mix, and grow. I thought to myself, *this is going to be great.* I was not only going to the retreat with a fellow pastor's wife, I was going to make a lot of new friends and learn how to do what only the best of the best wives can do. Be careful what you pray for!

The hundred mile drive from Houston was pleasant. The other pastor's wife and I laughed and chatted about our families. It was relaxing to step out of our roles and just be who God created us to be. We were two people who loved God and who knew God loved us. In that car, for two hours, we were just children of God having fun—like ordinary people do.

We did talk about what we thought might happen at the retreat. Both of us wanted to meet and make friends with other women in situations similar to ours. We were giddy and excited. This was going to be a turning point in our relationships with others... we thought.

We arrived that evening to appetizers and games to get to know everyone. You could hear lots of laughter and excitement in the room. I knew I was in the right place. I thought, *this is going to be better than I expected*. I looked around to see who might be able to help me become the best pastor's wife ever. I listened to people and pondered who might be a good mentor for me. I went to bed that night a little uneasy, thinking, *will these other women realize how inexperienced I am in this role*? What if they ask me something that I don't know? At this point, my spiritual foundation was somewhat weak. I didn't even know if Hebrews was in the Old or New Testament. Oh, my goodness, I really didn't even know the bible.

The next morning, we went to our first session and were broken into groups. I noticed tears streaming from the eyes of one of the participants. The face of one of the women in my group turned red. She was getting angry as she talked about how a congregation had mistreated her husband. One of the other wives was not saying anything. I wondered, "What happened to her?" One after another, each one opened up about their heartaches and struggles. They got real, and I got reality!

As I'm writing this, I do not want you to think all of this is true for all pastors' wives at all times. This was a retreat for us to come and be ourselves and have safe conversations. Many may have been waiting all year for this. As a newcomer, I was shocked. I didn't know what to say in the group. This was not what I expected from the other wives. I thought everyone would have it together and I was going to learn from them. I didn't know what to do. Maybe you're also in a situation where you don't know what to do. Maybe you are the wife of a pastor and you're filled with mixed emotions right now and don't know how to manage your feelings. Maybe you're a church member and you're close to a pastor's wife. Perhaps, the pastor's wife has confided in you about her hurts and you don't know what to do to help her. What can you do? I felt inadequate to offer help. All I could do was listen.

Unwittingly, as I listened to these other women, I discovered it was therapeutic. I didn't have to fix the situation. What I was learning as a pastor's wife was that, in order to help others, I needed to quit trying to make everything right for them. There are many helpful modalities that rely on active listening. When you listen to a person, you affirm their value and acknowledge that their voice is worthy of being heard. In difficult situations, listening may be one of the ways you can love a person and help them. I didn't know what to do, but I listened, and that was the best thing I could do. I'm no counselor, but I did what a friend would do. I just listened.

The retreat did have counselors you could sign up to talk with about what was going on in your life and to help you handle it. So here I was, fresh, young, energetic, and excited about what was going on in my congregation. I was feeling confident with the connections and friends I was making at my home church. Now I was with wives who were seasoned but had run out of seasoning.

They had come to the retreat because they were having problems dealing with their role in the congregation they were serving. No other role in any other occupation puts pressure on the spouse like this one. There are a myriad of expectations placed upon a pastor's wife, and these women were spilling their guts about their experiences. There was a tsunami of hurt and pain flooding this retreat.

Some of the women were wearied by ministry and felt like they couldn't do everything that was expected of them. Others were upset with the gossip, comments about their kids, and their lack of connections with other women. Some were broken and experiencing depression, anger, guilt, and anxiety. Here's what was written on the subject in *Manhattan Mental Counseling*:

Living By Others' Expectations can breed anger and resentment. The saying goes: "Expectations are premeditated resentments." It doesn't just breed resentment in the person whose expectations we fail to meet – it breeds resentment in us, as well. When we deny our own desires in favor of the expectations of others, we are prone to become resentful or angry."[vii]

Allow me to be clear, that quote implies that not all the expectations of what it means to be a pastor's wife come from the congregation. Sometimes the expectations come from you. You may have a different upbringing, a different personality, different gifts than the next person. Some of what you expect or desire from yourself comes from your past experiences or from what others have told you about yourself. If you don't know who you are, somebody will tell you who to be. If you deny your desires and try to please others all the time, it doesn't matter if you are in a large church, medium church, or small church, you will feel frustrated and angry. Pogo once said; "We have met the enemy and they is us!"[viii] When the expectations of the congregation and your own expectations collide, that is when resentment and bitterness develop. Unless these expectations are openly talked about, they may lead us down a destructive path.

I wish I had known all this back then. I naively thought I had come to the retreat to have fun and get to know "got-it-all-together" wives and learn from them. I quickly discovered that the road that lay ahead would not be easy. There was no fast lane to get to where I needed to go to be effective. It looked like I needed to go back to school to learn what it meant to be a pastors' wife. I needed to study up on myself and others instead of being handed all the answers. I grew to realize the road isn't linear. It is more like up and down, hills and valleys. There is no Map Quest to get you there with simple directions. I just had to hope I could avoid some of the potholes in the road.

I had all kinds of mixed emotions during the retreat. I was excited at first and then became disappointed and confused. I thought, "Where is the seasoning?" As the other wife and I packed to leave, I remember thinking "What was that? Glad I don't have those issues!" I was thinking I had it all together. I was loving our congregation! They were loving me, loving my husband, loving my family. Everything was going great!

On the drive home, I suddenly realized that every wife had their own story to tell. The common theme was they were wives of pastors and they were struggling. I realized that every wife had different experiences, some good and some bad. They needed connections to be real and to tell their story. This retreat was a safe place to do so. What happens when you have no one to confide in? What happens when you hold it in? You either split off your feelings and stuff them down, withdraw, act out, medicate yourself, or engage in a dozen other unhealthy behaviors. These women were getting it out with a safe group. It was the healthy choice for them to do so. They needed other people who understood what they were going through. Most did not have anyone they could turn to.

In another Pastor's Wife Survey that involved many Protestant Churches, Lifeway Research found:

50% of the wives surveyed agreed that they are not willing to confide in others at church because their confidence had been betrayed too many times.

55% agreed there are not enough relationships where they can be themselves.

56% agreed they have too few relationships that make them feel emotionally connected with others.

More than half of the pastors' spouses polled by Lifeway had experienced church conflicts such as personal attacks (51%) or resistance to their spouse's leadership (72%).[ix]

Maybe, I decided, I wasn't as put together as I first thought. I admit that I needed an attitude adjustment. I had more in common with the ladies there than I first thought. You know the old scripture, "Do not judge or you too will be judged" (Matthew 7.1) and "Pride goes before destruction"? (Proverbs 16.18)

Guess what?

A few years later, I was at the annual Pastors' Wives Retreat, and I was the one in tears needing a safe place to talk and a shoulder to cry on! My husband had become the Senior Pastor of our church and that stirred up all kinds of emotions inside of me and more expectations from the congregation. What I learned back then at the retreat has helped me cope and grow throughout the years. More on that in Chapter Five.

What I'd like to help you understand in this chapter is that there is no single description or prescription of how a pastor's wife should act in every situation. When I went to that retreat, I didn't really need to discover how to be a pastor's wife as much as I needed to discover how to be a friend. As I wrote earlier, everyone is different, and every situation is different. Here's what I do know: Everybody Needs Somebody! I think a pastors' wives retreat is a great place to go to be renewed, restored, and make friends. Again, you need to retreat to be renewed. Retreat doesn't always mean backing up, it can mean preparing for what's next.

One of the greatest gifts God gives us is friends. Among my close friends is another pastor's wife. Pastors' wives are great friends to pastors' wives. They have probably "been there and done that." The book of Proverbs says, "As iron sharpens iron, so one person sharpens another" (Proverbs 27.17). She encourages me when I need encouragement and keeps me sharp. I do the same for her.

In my circle of friends are a couple of ladies who I consider mentors. They are gifted differently. One of my mentors and confidantes is full of wisdom. She has a heart for God and service. I know she will be honest and lovingly tell me the truth. Another dear friend, who is a trusted confidante, is passionate and fiery. She will always stand up for me and my family and has taught me to stand up for myself. I developed these relationships over the years, and I know I can go to them with anything and they will listen to me, love me, and not judge me.

I have several circles of friends that I get together with periodically. Some go to our church and some do not. I love and trust these ladies as well. I can count on them anytime. They also know they can count on me. I call these circles my WOW groups. Before my husband retired, I had different ladies over for a bible study called WOW, Women of the Word. I would open a bottle of wine, and we would have appetizers as we studied the bible and visited. My husband walked in during the last few minutes of one of our meetings and noticed we were all drinking wine. One of the ladies had just shared some private things in her life and she was in tears. He assumed the wine got the conversation flowing and renamed us WOW, Women of Wine.

I mention often in this book, that for me, it was vital to build relationships within our congregation. Fortunately, in my marriage, we have only been in two congregations, 20 years in one and 11 years in the other. It is probably easier to have a congregation that feels like family when you have lived with them for years.

The writer of Ecclesiastes 4. 9-10 said, "Two are better than one because they have a good return for their labor: if either of them falls down, one can help the other up." The wisest man in the world, Solomon, wrote those words, which were inspired by the Holy Spirit. When Jesus walked on this earth, He had 12 close disciples.

One of those disciples whom he previously called a friend betrayed Him. Perhaps one of your friends have betrayed or hurt you. Jesus knows what it means to be betrayed by a friend. But Jesus didn't stop having friends. If He needed friends, how much more do you?

God created you to be a people person. You might be saying, "But I'm not a people person." Let me let you in on a little secret—you came from people! You were created a people person. But whether you agree with this or not, you bring the presence of Jesus Christ to other people through who you are. Here's what I learned about friendship and about being the best pastor's wife I could be. Through everything that I am and become, I want to bring Glory to God. I want to serve Him with all of my being through every connection. Some of those connections are going to be looser than others. But I connect, because God created me for relationships and has connected me to Himself in Jesus Christ.

I learned that the best way I could connect to others was:

1. Recognize that I am connected to God as His child. I John 3.1 says, "See what great love the Father has lavished on us, that one should be called children of God! And that is what we are!" My Identity in Christ is the foundation of who I am. I am a child of God. Now, I don't need peoples' approval to have value. I am valued and loved by my heavenly Father, despite what anyone may think about me.

2. I am the wife of a man who is a pastor. I am connected to him and our children. I put boundaries around those connections and try to always put my family first.

3. Finally, I am like every other person in the church. I am connected to the church as a member who uses my gifts to glorify God and help others.

The problem, I have learned over the years, is not what people expect of me or how others act. It is in me recognizing and living who I am in Christ and how I surrender to him and serve him every day Behind the Collar.

Chapter 4

Sons of a Preacher Man (PK's)

We sprinkle the ants at home, not at church!

It was a Monday morning at 8:30 a.m. when I brought my five-year-old son to kindergarten at our church. I was about to open the door to the entrance, a large room with glass windows through which you could see inside and outside. I started to open the door, looked back, and saw my son with his pants down, peeing on the bushes. The people inside saw it as well.

I immediately grabbed my son's shoulder and quietly said, "What are you doing?"

He innocently replied, "Sprinkling the ants."

I calmly let him know, "We don't sprinkle the ants at church. We sprinkle the ants only at home." My boys learned to sprinkle the ants from their grandmother (on their father's side). This was a little trick she used for potty training.

That was the beginning of a young boy learning about expectations—that certain behaviors are not appropriate at church. Some behaviors you hide so people don't look down on you.

After he pulled his pants up, we walked into the building. A group of eleven parents were there, and they were all laughing. One man shook his head and said, "That's a PK for you." That was the first time I had ever heard that phrase. I wasn't sure what it meant. I thought it probably meant "peeing kindergartner." I soon learned that was a common phrase used to describe pastors' kids. Wikipedia defines PK as "The child of a preacher or pastor, although it may be used as a descriptive, it sometimes is used as a stereotype."[x]

I defined it as expectations that are often unrealistic and damaging. PK meant, to me and many people, that either the child was a little angel living up to the label or a little devil rebelling against the expectation. The bottom line is that it means there are unrealistic expectations about pastors' kids.

Some of these unrealistic expectations about PKs were and still are:

1. Behave perfectly all the time (this is especially true in smaller churches)
2. Believe and know the bible well
3. Be happy and friendly all the time
4. Be a leader

5. Be careful what you say in public

I call these the "5 killer b's." You can find various versions of these in articles on expectations of pastors' kids. Pertinent to my situation, I would like to add one more that is not a "b" but a "d." Number six, Do not pee on the bushes in front of the church.

My boys were good, but let's face it—they were not perfect. No one ever said, "Your boys remind me of Jesus." Instead, for a long time, I would hear "That's the boy who peed in the bushes at the entrance of the church." Sometimes labels stick with you.

Jesus said, "Let the little children come to me" (Matthew 19.14). I believe He also would have said, "You over there sprinkling the ants. When you get through, come to me." As a parent, I needed that kind of Savior, and I have one.

My two boys went to church school, one for four years and the other for five years. They were smart, friendly, talented, and loved sports. They had many friends, and only occasionally did they get into trouble.

The dichotomy between behavior at home (real) and behavior at church (unreal) is a problem. On the one hand, I wanted my kids to respect others and learn appropriate behavior in public and in private. On the other hand, I did not want to teach my children to be hypocrites—to have a church face and behavior only when we were in church.

Jesus got upset with the Pharisees because that is what they did. They put on a "religious face and church behavior." From the outside, they looked admirable, but on the inside, they were like "white-washed tombs" (Matthew 23:27).

George Barna, the great church researcher, found in one of his studies that PKs were just as normal as anyone but resisted having a church face and a home face.[xi] In the words of my five-year-old, they wanted to feel comfortable being real at church, "sprinkling the ants."

I had no idea that some church people were twofaced. However, it finally dawned on me that some people in church acted one way on Sunday and another on Monday. Somebody said, "People go to church on Sunday and act like saints, but on Monday act like the devil." Being called a PK, in my mind seemed to reinforce this twofaced behavior. It meant that you must hide how you really feel and act at church. At home and everywhere else, you do what you always do.

So, over the years, I have sat down with my kids and talked with them about this. I wanted to assure them that their dad and I loved them unconditionally, seven days a week. I wanted them to know they could be themselves in church. They did. One of the fun things they would do after church is get their vitamin C. On communion Sundays, while the elders were putting away communion, our boys would disappear. I would find them in the sacristy with the elders who would be handing them shot glasses of grape juice that were left over. In our church, we use real wine for communion wine but also have grape juice for those unable to have alcohol. They would each down about twenty plus shots of grape juice.

Here are nine things that our kids and other pastors' kids in my research have said they need from their parents:

1. Affirm us. Use words that build up not tear us down (be our cheerleader).
2. Tell us you love each other and show us a happy marriage (provide security).
3. Spend time with us (love for many kids is spelled T.I.M.E.).
4. Treat us as normal kids. We are not "mini-pastors." We are not "holy children" (we love you and need you to help us grow).
5. Don't use us for illustrations in your sermons (we get embarrassed).
6. If we pee on the bushes, gently remind us of what we should be doing and show us grace (correct us in private).
7. Treat us as kids not small adults (we are growing and need your protection).
8. Don't give us a Christmas present called "Preach and Play" with an altar, pulpit, and microphone (we don't want to be forced to be pastors).

9. Don't leave us because you have a meeting (show us we're important).

Which of these needs from parents do you think your children need? Perhaps your kids need the same thing as everyone else.

Labels can lead someone to exceed or become the negative part of the label. People, especially children, tend to live out expectations they have for themselves and from others.

In the midst of all this, there were times when I felt like I was not a good parent. Have you ever felt that way? I had my doubts and wondered if I was cut out for this motherly role.

My husband and I had been married eight years when I discovered I was pregnant. I had grown up taking care of younger siblings and babysitting for younger cousins who were difficult. I felt quite certain I was not interested in having children. I thank God that He had another plan for my life. It included two boys. I remember the Sunday morning when my husband announced that we were going to have a baby. The congregation erupted with loud cheers and clapping! My husband walked over to where I was sitting in the pew and gave me a beautiful, blooming, white azalea tree. We were so excited, and the church was excited for us. The ladies got together and hosted one of the largest baby showers I had ever attended. We got everything and more than we would need to have a baby.

Our son Taylor was born a few weeks later. Wow, that was something for which no one can prepare you. It was miraculous! I had no idea I could love someone so much. I got a glimpse of how much God must love His children. In the midst of all my excitement and this deep love, I honestly had no idea of what lay ahead. You may remember I had done a lot of babysitting in my youth and I had a negative attitude toward having children. Yet this was different. This was the deepest love I had ever felt for someone else… my child.

When we were released from the hospital, I faced the reality of not knowing what to do. This was not like babysitting someone else's child, this was *my* child. They did not give me a set of instructions before I left the hospital. I had read the book prior to delivery, *What to Expect When You're Expecting*, but what about what to expect after you deliver? I was on my own. Raising a newborn was not like babysitting. I could not leave after a few hours. It was exhausting! Our child was colicky. I called the hospital to see if I could come with my baby and stay another day or two? Really, that's true! They wouldn't let me. I needed some help. I didn't know what to do. Thank God for a grandmother and a godmother who came and rescued us. After two nights of my son crying at home, my son's godmother, Virginia, actually burped him for the first time. My grandmother came to help and lived with us for several months. I felt I could now breathe a little.

I don't know what happened to all my confidence, but I turned into a "nervous nelly" mom. My son survived. We survived and were starting to get the hang of this parenting thing. I was feeling better about everything, and my figure was even returning. My grandmother who was living with us saw me in a tight red dress and warned me, "You better not wear that. You just might get pregnant again." She must have been a prophetess. I got pregnant again.

I'm sad to say, I wasn't as excited as I was the first time I found out I was pregnant. It is hard to be excited when you still feel exhausted. I also didn't think I was a "naturally good mom." Again, maybe my expectations for myself were too high. It didn't help that we lived 20 miles from church, and in traffic it took a good hour for my husband to get home. I started feeling like a single parent. I needed a break.

Just before our second child was born, God blessed us with a corner lot close to the church. We built a beautiful home. It was small, but perfect for us. I told my husband I would live in a shoe box if we could move close to church. It had a porch on the front and a porch on the back. We loved it and have such great memories there.

I was so thankful. Thankful for a new home that was 5 miles away from church and in traffic 5 to 7 minutes away from church. Thankful for a beautiful, healthy baby boy and his seventeen-month-old big brother. Thankful that my husband (their dad) could come home for lunch or dinner! In the early days, I would have been so excited to see him because I adored him, but this day I was so thankful to see him because I knew he would love on and look after our boys and I would have a break. I was thankful that I was able to stay home with the boys. I wouldn't trade that time for anything. I just needed some personal time away.

Honestly, Behind the Collar, I knew I was not Mary raising Jesus. I must admit my kids were never perfect. My youngest went to the principal's office a few times. The first time it was for accepting a challenge to stand on the sink in the boy's restroom. He got caught. While it was not a capital offense with the death penalty, it was serious since, as the principal said, "He is a PK and should be a role model for the other kids."

The next time, he was in the office for chewing gum in the hall. In a church school, this was almost punishable by stoning. However, they just called my husband to the principal's office and they "worked it out." Little offenses mean a lot to some people when the offender is a PK.

Here is what God taught me about "PKs." The bible says children are a gift from God. They are like "arrows in your quiver" (Psalm 127.5). God gives them to you because He wants you to raise them to be light and salt in this world, to bring the Kingdom of God by their life and their witness. They are not perfect, and you are not either. In the bible, even Adam and Eve struggled with their kids, one of which killed the other (Genesis 4.8).

Instead of saying to myself, my kids should be perfect. I learned to say to myself, "I would prefer that they behave better, but they are only children." I learned to treat them as individuals with needs. I treated my boys as people who had God-given dreams and talents. I taught them that our God is a good, good Father. I learned to forgive myself and to move on from my mistakes. I am not the best parent in the world, but I am the best I can be. I may parent differently than you, but my kids turned out okay. I asked my son to write a letter about being a pastor's kid. I asked him to be truthful, however; I was a little nervous about "the whole truth and nothing but the truth so help me God." This is what he wrote.

Being a pastor's kid

Growing up being a pastor's son, I believe I learned a lot of valuable life lessons. Of these lessons, the one that stuck with me the most was how to treat everyone with love and truly care about every single person I come in contact with. Since I was a kid, my family consistently provided me with good examples of this, such as going out of our way to feed/shelter the homeless, along with spreading the word of god to them, to my dad sacrificing time with his own family to pray for people who are terminally ill or going through a rough patch in their life. I specifically remember an incident when I was in high school. I got a sales call to my cell phone and I remember cursing at the caller and hanging up on them. The next day while we were eating dinner, my dad's cell phone rings, and he got up to take it, excusing himself to the living room where we hear him sharing a bible verse and then praying for the person on the phone for what seemed like 5-10 minutes! When he came back to the table, we asked who he was talking to and he replied, "they had the wrong number." That is just how my dad is, but I believe I got to see many more examples of showing compassion for people due to my dad being a pastor and being extremely involved in the church.

I think being able to witness this type of care for others is partially what drove my decision to become a firefighter and paramedic.

Growing up being a pastor's son, I believe I had an extremely large support group (the church) of all different ages and backgrounds. This led to me being fortunate enough to get a summer job doing general maintenance with Brick Scott, a friend from church, at the golf course which really showed me the value of hard work and what I had in store for me as I grow up. In my later high school years and early college years I remember constantly having at least 3 mentor/teacher figures inviting me to lunch, dinner, or even just to hang out. Most of the time I didn't accept, but looking back, it was really cool for them to genuinely care about me when I had done nothing but decline their offers. Which leads me to the part of my life where I went through the typical pastor's son rebellious phase. I still consider this a positive part of my life because aside from it being extremely fun, I believe I learned to truly relate and be friends with more of the "rough" crowd, which I think puts me in a unique position to spread the word of God or even just be a further example of how to treat others. I will say that had I not had such a huge support group from my family and from the church, my life would have turned out completely different. During these years, I remember experimenting with quite a few different drugs as well as committing many other minor offences. All throughout this time, I came home and would start arguments with my family that would always be met with a bible verse or a well put together calmness from my dad (not so much my mom). I think if I had been my own parent through this time, I would have kicked myself out. But instead, I had multiple church members, specifically the mentors I mentioned earlier, reach out and offer to just listen to me without judgement, which is really what I needed at the time!

As for the negatives, growing up, everything I just mentioned seemed like a negative, but looking back on it, they turned out to be all positives. There are a couple of truly negative things about being a pastor's kid. One is that there are a lot more people watching what you do and making sure I was accountable for everything I had done. The other is that growing up, there was never a question of if we were going to church or not , it was 100% attendance pretty much, and as a kid, I really didn't want to go to church a lot of the time. I think this made me view going to church as a chore, and even though I have kind of grown out of that phase, I still do not attend as often as I should. Altogether, I am extremely grateful for growing up as a pastor's kid and believe that it has made me the man I am today.

Short version - positives:

Always had a big support group

More opportunities than most

More exposure to different age groups and cultures

More opportunities for life lessons

Negatives: view church as a chore

More people watching what I do

Higher expectations in general

Love, Taylor

By the way, there is a 50 percent chance that he was the one who "sprinkled the ants." He is real. He is faithful. And I am proud of him. He is not a label. He is my son, and as the apostle John wrote, "I have no greater joy than to hear that my children are walking in the truth" (3 John 1.4).

Perhaps you are dealing with the label PK for your kids, or perhaps you're a kid dealing with the label PK. If you are a church member, perhaps you are realizing that this label generalizes and may invite rebellious behavior. "Pastor's kid" is not a job title. In any case, I suggest you begin to see the pastor's kids, or yourself if you are a PK, as God's Kids—"GKs!" GKs are just as normal as anyone else. They have the same needs as other kids. They want you to treat them like anyone else.

I keep saying, "If you can, make the congregation your family." In the church, we are the family of God. When you are raising children who happen to be children of the pastor, it is helpful if you have a church family to help you raise them. It takes a village to raise a child. One of the greatest things a church family can do for the family Behind the Collar is to love the pastor's kids and treat them like anyone else's kids. Thankfully, we were part of two special congregations that did exactly that. They covered our kids with love and grace. Instead of unrealistic expectations, they accepted my kids as regular kids. That happened because the congregation became our family, and they truly loved us.

Jesus never turned away children or stereotyped them. He loved them. I urge you to treat the pastor's kids as normal, like anyone else's children, and welcome them as Jesus did, even when they "sprinkle the ants."

Chapter 5

Should I Stay or
Should I Go

The realization didn't come overnight, but one day it dawned on me that I could no longer live Behind the Collar with this man. Once, I thought he was my Prince Charming and I was Cinderella. But the glass slipper was the wrong size. The shoe didn't fit. Now the senior pastor at a large church, my husband was going to the top, but I was sinking to the bottom. His over involvement in the church was taking a toll on me.

The role of a pastor's wife was not only challenging, it was also emotionally draining. I started out starry eyed, but as the reality of my situation came crashing down, I became sad eyes. There is a hymn in one of our hymnals called, O' Day of Rest and Gladness. For me, Sunday was O' Day of Mess and Madness. Every Sunday, my husband was at church by 7:00 a.m. to prepare for the 8:00 a.m. service. I was left to get the rest of the family ready. Most of the time, I had to make breakfast, dress the boys, and get myself ready as well.

Often, I would make sure the house was clean and prepare lunch in case we invited friends or newcomers over. I would get to church early in case something needed to be done last minute or I had some responsibility to take care of. By that time, I was usually frazzled.

After a few years of ups and downs, I gave up. I threw in the towel and walked away. I left my husband and moved out. I took both boys and moved back to my hometown in East Texas. It had been a long time coming, but I finally decided it was what I needed to do.

Some pastors' wives throw in the towel more subtly. They keep up appearances but inside they are dying. They can't handle the lack of connection—spousal connection, family connection, social connection. They feel they are unfairly criticized. Some begin to lose their sense of self. They are tired of playing church. Their family is not perfect, but many in congregations expect the pastor's family to be extra holy. The judgement lands on their shoulders if they fail at this. Perhaps you have experienced this and are nodding along with my assessment of the situation.

Every pastor's wife has scars. They may not admit it. They may say, "Just trust Jesus more. It will be alright." The truth is, this role can be tough. We need to be honest with ourselves about the difficulties. I have learned the price of being dishonest with myself and others. At some point, I began to "act" the role of pastor's wife to meet expectations. I thought others had it altogether while I was failing. I tried harder, but this only made me angry, discouraged, and resentful.

For a long time, everything in our life was going so well! My husband was the associate pastor in a church that had 3 pastors. We had just had our second child. We were about to move into our new home, which was close to the church. Everything had been close to perfect, when five church officers invited my husband to a breakfast meeting. They wanted to make him the senior pastor because the senior pastor that he had worked for all these years was going on disability with a bad back.

My husband loved that pastor who had stood up for him on more than a few occasions and taught him to stand up to people. He had mentored my husband with love and grace. My husband informed the church officers that he did not want to be senior pastor. We were about to move into a new home, we had a new baby, and he was not sure he was up to the job. The church officers insisted he would be a perfect fit for the job and there was no one else to do it. They discussed it, and my husband agreed to a trial period of one year.

One of wonderful things about my husband is that when he is put in charge of 'something,' he takes that charge very seriously. He learns as much as he can and gives one hundred percent of himself to that 'something.' So, yes, of course he could do the job, and he was good at it! Some of our church members called him, "progressive, cutting edge." He hit the ground running. Everyone already knew him from his time as the associate, and really liked him.

My husband began to set up goals and strategies. He worked with 30 elders to plan the work and work the plan. He sought out a mentor who was the senior pastor of a sister congregation down the road. Through this mentoring, he established a Board of Directors. He also worked closely with the Board of Elders; whose role was to assist the pastors in caring for the congregation. I thought the Board of Directors was a great idea. Everything would not solely fall on his shoulders. Or so I thought. Somehow, the responsibility was still large since he was working with both boards.

He had always been a wonderful preacher and teacher. Now, as senior pastor, he did most of the preaching. The congregation embraced his leadership. He loved this role. It was challenging, but my husband had always loved a challenge. He was a natural born leader, a visionary with a knack for leading and motivating people. He provided training for the staff, elders, and the boards. He also began to oversee worship planning. Worship was exciting.

God was doing amazing things in our church. It was growing. We went from two services to three services plus a youth service in the gym. As the church and the school grew, the responsibilities increased. More staff were hired. I believe the church staff, along with the school staff, numbered over one hundred. It was the best and worst of times.

The position was demanding more of both of us than I had expected. While my husband, Bill, was pouring his time and energy into moving the church ahead, I was feeling overwhelmed and disappointed. Overwhelmed by the pace at which everything was moving for him at church and disappointed with how that pace was affecting him at home. By now, we lived close to the church and he could come home for lunch or dinner. And he often did, only to pass out on the sofa from exhaustion.

I looked forward to him coming home. I was hungry for some adult conversation. I also wanted him to spend some quality time with the kids. When at home, he would try hard to be a good husband and a good dad, but he was tired, mentally and physically. I felt guilty if I complained because being able to stay home with the kids was a gift, and I was thankful for it. Meanwhile, he was working hard to make a difference for the church and the Kingdom of God. How could I hold that against him?

Still, he had become an absentee dad and husband. His excuse was, "I'm working." His sole focus was on growing the church. I began to resent him and the church. The boys and I had become low on the priority list. I vented some of this frustration one evening when he called to tell me he would be coming home late. That day, a pastor from the California District had come to visit our church and do some training. My husband had spent the day there with him. They had also gone to dinner that evening. Following dinner, my husband and this pastor met with the Board of Elders and the Board of Directors.

Then I got the phone call. I assumed he was finally coming home. But no. The call was to let me know he and this district pastor were going out for a drink. I lost it! I rattled off a few words not appropriate to share! In the background, I heard the voice of the other pastor say, "Looks like you better go home." To my horror, I realized I was on speaker phone! That was a reality check. I had taken things too far.

The best way to not get what you want is to never ask for it. I didn't ask my husband for what I needed from him. I didn't tell him I was struggling, that I was drowning in this despondency. This was something I could not share with anyone. Even though this church was like my family, it felt too risky to let them know what was going on. I was afraid of what they would think of me, and what they might do to him. I guarded these feelings so closely that my own husband didn't even know. I just kept smiling and going through the motions, day after day. My desperation grew until it became greater than my fear. Finally, I let my husband know what was going on. But by then, I already had one foot out the door.

My husband suggested I talk to the head of Stephen Ministry. Stephen Ministry is a lay caring ministry that my husband started at our church. He personally had trained leaders, who trained lay people, to go out and care for others in times of need. They were not cure givers. They were care givers. I arranged a lunch with the leader. I told her I needed to talk to someone about something very important. We met for lunch. Once I worked up the nerve to tell her I was thinking about leaving my husband, I don't think she ate another bite. She was shocked. I had worn the happy wife mask so well, no one had ever suspected.

After our discussion, I still felt like I needed to go. Inside, a part of me was angry. I didn't know who I was or what I was meant to be doing.

My husband also suggested we go to counseling. I was not real excited about that. My husband has his doctorate in counseling, and I knew he could verbally run circles around me. I was sure that was not going to help this situation, so I told him I just had to get away. I had to breathe. I was broken, I had such a heaviness in me. Maybe it was so heavy because I had let it pile up on me. I only knew I wanted to go home, to be close to my family, to work and be normal (whatever that is). I didn't want to call it a separation because I still loved him, and he loved me. We remained committed to each other.

But I was going to go, there was no changing my mind. I wrote the elders a letter to let them know about my plans. I still have it tucked away in my devotional book. This is what it said:

Dear St. Mark Elders,

I know this letter will be hard for you to read, but it's even harder for me to write. St. Mark has been my family for fifteen years, and it hurts my heart to tell you this; I asked Bill for a separation this summer! Our marriage, from my point of view, has deteriorated over the past three years, and I have reached the point where I need to get away and take some time to clear my head and not be influenced by Bill. I'm having a hard time distinguishing my thoughts from his.

Bill has not been a bad father or a bad husband. He has worked hard at both, but I feel he has worked a lot harder at being the senior pastor of St. Mark. I know he feels called to lead our church, and I think he has done a great job, but it has taken its toll on our family. When he did make time for us, he was already used up from work, and that made matters worse. I'm not blaming him. I should have stood up and let him know how I felt three years ago, and we probably would have taken care of this then. However, I let things continue, and now our relationship is in trouble.

I know this goes against everything Bill and I stand for. I know he loves me and wants to work this out. We attended a marriage workshop this summer, and we saw a counselor and will continue to do so. I need the time away to re-affirm some things and heal some hurts.

The last thing I want to do is hurt our church and our children. Please understand my decision and keep Bill, myself, Taylor, and Tristen in your prayers.

Your sister in Christ,

Sheila Dasch

Not long after the announcement of our separation, one of the associate pastors came up to my husband and said, "I think you should consider not preaching during this time." With this, you again see an expectation, not only of pastors' wives, but of a pastor himself; that his family should always be great and strong and never have any issues. My husband responded, "I'll let the Board of Directors and Elders decide that." The decision was that he could still preach, but not as much, and the other associates would step up to preach more. After all, we were not divorced, just separated. The church stood by and supported and prayed for us. They did not remove him from leadership. But it was a sad time.

I moved back to my hometown and set up house. I got a job at my uncle's title company. It was a peaceful transition. I enrolled the boys in public school. Taylor was in the second grade and Tristen was a kindergartner. The changes were especially hard on them. I had always been told kids were resilient and adjusted more easily to change than adults, but this did not seem to be the case. I, on the other hand, felt like this heavy load had been lifted from my shoulders. I was happy to be at a place with no expectations and no judgement. A place where I had grown up. My family lived here. I thought seeing their grandma and spending time with their cousins would give the boys a sense of "family" and "security."

On my third day of work, I got a phone call from the President of the Texas District, Jerry Kieschnick. He wanted to know how the boys and I were doing. He also wanted to know why I left. I told him the same thing I'd told my husband, the same thing I'd written in the letter to the elders; "Bill was a better senior pastor than he was a dad and husband." He asked the question, which every district president has to ask when a pastor and wife separate, "Was there any infidelity on your husband's part?" I assured him there was not. I cannot remember if he asked me about infidelity on my part, but I assure you, there was none of that either. This was about me needing to get out from Behind the Collar. The collar was choking me! For my mental health, I needed to step away for a while. At the time, I did not realize all the ramifications and the questions surrounding a pastor's wife's departure.

The church knew very little about what was going on. Thankfully, those who did know something, did not take sides. There were people from church who called me and kept up with me. They said they would stand by and pray for both me and my husband. Their check-ins were invaluable to me. This is why I say make the congregation your family. Allow them to love on you.

That's what families do. You are not like a family. You are a family. We are brothers and sisters in Christ.

One of the conditions to which Bill and I agreed was that I would bring the boys back on weekends when my husband could not come see us. Since it was still hard for him to get away on weekends, I often brought the kids to him. One of the weekends that we visited my husband, he had planned a big birthday party for one of the boys. He invited everyone special to them. When our son, Taylor, saw his godmother, Virginia, he was so happy. He ran to her, threw his arms around her legs, and buried himself in her stomach. That was the first time I saw true joy in him since we had left. I made the decision that day to come back home. I left the boys there so they could return to their old school the following Monday. I went back to my hometown, put in my two weeks' notice at my job, and then returned home to my husband and my boys.

It's funny how God works. We had gone to counseling during our separation. I don't think it was helpful for me. I am not saying counseling can't help—I recommend it for many situations—I am saying, I don't think it helped in my situation. I was already convinced that what I needed was time to sort things out. But when I saw the joy on my son's face when he was back with his friends and "church family," I knew God was showing me what I needed. It was time to come home. Time to deal with our issues.

Looking back, I wished I would have called this a sabbatical instead of a separation. I had returned home in less than 2 months. This really was time away, a breather, time to reflect, restore, and renew.

Maybe God used this as a wakeup call. My husband stopped taking me for granted. I stopped taking him for granted as well and started talking about my feelings with him. He started investing emotionally in our family, as well as investing his time. Our church also held him accountable for taking time for his family. I learned that I could not count on my husband to give me everything I need. I needed to count on Jesus, who supplies all my needs. I moved from religion which is a set of rules and behaviors to relationship, which is a connection to God's love and His forgiveness, for me and all people.

I had played my role so well; my faith became outward compliance. Shaunti Feldhahn wrote *The Surprising Secrets of Highly Happy Marriages*. She found that the secret to Highly Happy Marriages was that highly happy couples put God at the center of their marriage. She explained, "Highly happy couples tend to put God at the center of their marriage and focus on Him, rather than their marriage or spouse for fulfillment and happiness."[xii]

Here are practical characteristics of putting God at the center of your marriage:

1. They attend church nearly every week.
2. They read their bibles daily.
3. They read spiritual material regularly.
4. They pray privately and together.
5. They are not perfect people, but they are committed.
6. These committed people generally have happy marriages.

In the majority of cases, she found that the common element in highly happy couples was faith commitment, putting Jesus at the center. Jesus makes the difference. If a couple grows together toward Jesus Christ, they also grow toward each other.

Some of my friends call me Dr. Love because I once called in to a talk radio show to answer a question they were asking. They asked, "What is the best advice or wisdom you can give to newly married couples?" I was driving on the freeway and had to pull over so I could call. I wanted them to know what I'm telling you as well. I said, "Love doesn't keep a marriage together. Marriage and the commitment you make keep love together. Every marriage has ups and downs, but if you stay committed to each other, you will get through them." That love and commitment come from the God who created you, loves you, and is committed to you.

I discovered my spouse is not my savior. Jesus is. In the gospel of John, chapter 2, Jesus and his disciples were invited to a wedding at Cana in Galilee. When the wine ran out at the reception, Jesus turned water into wine. Most scholars agree that he made more than 600 fifths of fine wine (I bet it was a Cabernet). Now that's a wedding present! Invite Him into your marriage and get ready for what He brings. He always brings the best.

Today, as I was finishing up this chapter, I spoke with my husband about what we had gone through. We got up from the table to make lunch, and out of nowhere, our Alexa suddenly came on and said, "Shuffling songs by Louis Armstrong." My husband and I looked at each other with surprise. Then she started playing "What a Wonderful World." Our mouths fell open. How did that happen? We both had chills and goose bumps as we heard the words to that song "What a Wonderful World."

In the beginning, God made a wonderful world. A great marriage is a glimpse of the wonder He put in the world. Marriage is His idea. He put the first couple together in the Garden of Eden. You need your spouse. He needs you. Most of all, you need your God who created you with your needs. He will strengthen your marriage and lead you in the right direction. When you include Him in your marriage, you can live happily ever after.

I am glad I came back. I am glad I came home. My prayer is that you have learned from my brokenness and my journey and it will help your marriage Behind the Collar.

Chapter 6

Don't Be Cruel

One of the greatest challenges I found Behind the Collar was dealing with criticism. Sometimes it was criticism about me, but more often it was criticism of my husband or my children. Brian Jones recently wrote in an article, "The one thing Senior Pastors have in common is that we are all constant targets for critics."[xiii] Earlier, Thom Ranier wrote an article, "7 Things Pastors' Wives Wish They Had Been Told." In an informal survey, he asked pastors wives what they wished they had known before taking on their role. Their responses were listed in the order of frequency. Number two on this list was criticism. One wife said, "I wish someone would have prepared me to deal with criticism of my husband and me. It was hard to deal with negative experiences, conflicts, or criticisms, especially in relation to my husband and our area of ministry. I began to harbor feelings of resentment when it came to ministry and my man."[xiv]

Every pastor's wife must come to terms with criticism. There are no exceptions. Criticism, however, was not the major problem in my life or the churches we were in, partially because, as we've discussed in previous chapters, these churches became second families to my husband and me. The strong relationships we forged with other members of the Church eased some of the burden— people were less inclined to criticize purely out of spite. But it was present in our lives. There will always be natural gossips and those with differing opinions, even in a healthy church. At times, it can seem to be suffocating. When criticism did rear its head, I experienced a range of emotions from anger to disappointment and even discouragement.

You have heard the old saying "sticks and stones may break my bones, but words will never hurt me." These words are far from the truth. Words can bless or curse people. Words are powerful. They can injure people. The bible says, "The tongue has the power of life and death" (Proverbs 18.21). Not everyone heeds what the apostle Paul wrote in Ephesians 4.29, "Use words that build up, not tear down." After Sunday service, some have roast pastor for lunch.

It took me a while to realize that some people felt like they had the spiritual gift of criticism and were more than willing to share it. Perhaps right now you are nodding your head in agreement because you have experienced criticism of yourself or your spouse and family. You love your husband and your family and your church, yet, you are frustrated by the criticism that has come against you or your family. Jesus said, "You will know the truth and the truth will set you free." The truth is that you cannot please everyone. Not everyone is going to like you. Even Jesus could not please his critics, and they crucified him for it—literally.

When my husband was an associate pastor, everyone loved him. He was the fair-haired child of the congregation. Blessings and success seemed to follow him wherever he went. There were few, if any, critics. But, when he became the Senior Pastor, even while the church was experiencing dynamic growth, critics crawled out of the woodwork. No matter how good you are, someone will find something to criticize you about.

My husband was exceptionally good at what he did. He strategically started laying the foundation to move the church forward. With the help and support of the Church Officers and Board of Directors, he created a vision and mission for the church. He asked the tough questions, "Why are we here?" "Who can we reach?" "How do we reach them?" and "What needs to change?" That was the kicker. Few wanted to change!

My husband worked with the worship team to institute changes to one of the services. The 8:00 a.m. service remained traditional. The 10:45 service became a blended praise and worship service. The goal of the second service was to reach a different demographic that was not traditional Lutheran. He wanted to make worship exciting! It wasn't long before we added a third worship service. We were starting to outgrow the building and, in turn, silence the criticisms.

He worked diligently to get everyone on board. He took small steps to gain full support. He was aware that there would be some resistance to change. He attempted to take things slowly. However, his idea of slow was not the same as other people's. They didn't like slow, they wanted "whoa."

It takes courageous leadership to move a large church forward. For the most part, many in church were onboard and supported his leadership. A few left the church. That was hard for me. I was passionate about our church, and being a people pleaser, I wanted everyone to be happy and love our church as much as I did. My husband, who doesn't need to please everyone, informed me that it's okay for people to leave. He said to me, "It doesn't mean they are lost to the Kingdom; they may need a church that better fits them." It was still hard to watch those I considered 'family' go somewhere else. I took it personally.

I wondered if people realized how far the church had come due to the changes we had made? Were they looking at all the things they had lost instead of all the great things they had gained? We were rising to become one of the top Lutheran Churches in America. Our worship attendance reached an all-time high, as did our bible attendance, and our church school attendance mushroomed. Things were going well, but it had been a rocky road. It was like juggling knives; you could be cut at any moment.

Every pastor has been cut at some time. I remember one Monday morning when my husband and I walked into a restaurant to have breakfast. Sitting near the front was a table of local pastors. My husband asked them what they were all doing there together. A Baptist preacher replied, "This is where we come and lick our wounds from Sunday's critics."

Few people realize what many pastors go through. They are not walking a yellow brick road. They are the ones who make the tough decisions. The responsibility rests on their shoulders, and their church rises or falls based on their decisions. They handle all the problems of the church, whether they created them or not. Someone once said, "He who calls the shots, takes the shots." My husband had a tee shirt with deer antlers on it that said, "The buck stops here." I think there were some discontents who wanted to "shoot the buck."

For many years, I thought all church people were unified in the mission of bringing in the Kingdom of God. I thought that everyone would approve of what a growing church was doing. I was wrong. The church is full of people, all kinds of people, with all kinds of flaws. The apostle Paul wrote in I Corinthians 4, "We have this treasure in clay pots." The term clay pots refer to the people in church. Some people are chipped pots, broken pots, and some are crack pots. Clay pots are often weak and brittle, but the church is not about perfect people. It never has been. It is not a museum for saints. It is a hospital for sinners. It is a place for the weak to be made strong. I'm glad, because sometimes I felt like kicking the clay pot.

How do you handle criticism when it's aimed at your husband and you can't fight back? Over time, I began to understand the criticism says more about the person doing the criticizing than it does about the person they are criticizing. Criticism can sometimes be constructive. Be open to it and be able to discern how and if it fits your situation. Learn what works for you. My husband would say, "You can always have your say, but you may not always have your way." He would listen to people but felt free to disagree with them.

Unique to the church at large is the fact that people who have no power anywhere in their life can express their frustration at church. They feel powerless at home or work, and they project their frustration at the church where they have a voice and power. No other organization would allow individuals to stand up and voice their criticism the way the church does. Most churches want to appease everyone. One complaining person can stop a whole meeting by simply standing up and saying, "I'm upset, and I don't agree." The whole meeting stops, and someone says, "Let's hear what you have to say. We want you to be happy. What can we do to please you?" They focus on the one unhappy person, instead of the others who are content and ready to move forward. Instead of saying thank you for sharing your grievance with us, they stop the meeting and focus on the critic rather than continuing with the agenda.

Many churches have a default complaint department. It usually is the president, vice president of the board, and the board of elders. These are the people the complainers go to when they have a gripe about the church or the pastor or his family. While these positions were not originally designed to be complaint departments, they often unwittingly become just that. The people in these positions fall into the trap of listening to complaints, and may even begin to believe them. This puts the person in office in an adversarial position. Instead of directing the complainer to the person they are complaining about, they unintentionally triangulate against the pastor and his family.

What is triangulation? Imagine a triangle in front of you. At the bottom right is the complainer. At the bottom left is the chairman of the board of the elders. At the top is the pastor. Instead of going to the pastor, the complainer goes to the chairman. The goal of triangulation is to ease the anxiety of the complainer. Triangulation occurs when a person lacks the courage to bring their grievance to the person he has a problem with and instead talks to everyone else. This is better known as gossip. The Bible is clear about how to handle personal conflict. Jesus said, "If your brother or sister sins go and point out their fault, just between the two of you" (Matthew 18.15). It does not say "go and tell all your friends."

In my head, I've always known criticism comes with the territory. In my heart, I had a problem with it. I remember a time when my husband had to let one of the longtime staff go. Many people were upset and wanted his head. He could not let the general congregation know the circumstances that surrounded this release. It was kept confidential to protect the staff member. On the other hand, if the congregation had found out what the staff member was involved in and my husband had turned a blind eye and let it go, then the church would have probably let my husband go. It was a catch-22 in my opinion.

I learned that in some cases, you must make hard decisions even if others do not approve or know all the facts. Being a leader means you hope for everyone's approval, but you don't need it, as long as you are doing the right thing. My husband was much better suited for this than I.

People can also be critical because they do not perceive things in the way that you intended. I recall visiting with a friend after church one Sunday. One of the church members walked up and, right in front of me, told my friend that Pastor Dasch had kicked her and her husband out of the late service. I wondered if she forgot I was married to him. I had to say something to set the record straight. I nicely replied, "That's not how I remember it. He invited you to attend the earlier service, since this one was upsetting you." I was a little fired up, but I treated her with respect and kindness.

Sometimes, just speaking up and clarifying the situation can pacify a critic. Proverbs 15.1 says, "A gentle answer turns away wrath, but a harsh word stirs up anger." The pulpit commentary explained this verse saying, "Not only should the answer be gentle and conciliatory, but you should not be silent." A bit of confession here; the older I get, the harder I find it to remain silent in the face of unjust criticism.

I have also heard criticism from ladies who I thought were my friends. I was regularly invited to pool day with the girls. We would swim, have lunch, and talk about things that were going on at the church. I later learned from a close friend that when I couldn't make it to a pool day, the talk centered around me and my husband. Over time, I've learned to consider the source. These weren't bad people, just natural 'gossipers' (James 1.26). There were other occasions when people would talk to me about things they did not like about the church. They were trying to use me as a sounding board in the hopes I would pass on their complaints to my husband. When this happened, I cordially let them know that I would be happy to set up a time for them to speak with my husband personally about their issues.

I learned a particular type of dialogue works great when critics are intent on finding fault. You simply repeat back to the person what they have said. This helps with clarity, and it also causes you to slow down and listen. After you have echoed their thoughts, you validate what they have said. For example: "...that makes sense because ..." and lastly, you show empathy, "...I can imagine you feel...". You can read more about "Handling Criticism" in the Appendix.

I now understand that the way I handle conflict has a lot to do with how I feel about myself. When you know who you are, you are less likely to be swayed by the opinions of others. You are a child of God, and you have value. If you are self-controlled and deflect criticism, your critics cannot talk down to you. My grandma use to say, "You catch more flies with honey than with vinegar." Critical people in the church are not your enemies. They are brothers and sisters in Christ with different opinions. Learn to speak to them gently and with respect, listen to them and do not cut them off. Sometimes, they have something valuable to say. That is why you must consider whose voice is important to you. If God has called on you to do something and someone complains when you do it, consider whose voice you value more—God's or the critic's? A banner on the wall of a church said, "There will come a time when our love for God is greater than our fear of people."

Because I am forgiven by God in Jesus Christ and His death on the cross, I have learned to forgive. It did not come naturally to me, and it is not always easy. God's word says, "Bear with each other and forgive one another. Forgive as the Lord forgave you" (Colossians 3.13). This does not discount the offense against you, it simply reminds you of the grace God has shown you; "forgive as the Lord forgave you."

The forgiven are forgiving. So, when wounded by the words of others, I quietly uttered, "I forgive you" to the people who had hurt me and my family. It was a start. I also learned a forgiveness exercise, which you can find in the Appendix. Through this exercise, I let go of all my pain and hurt and forgave the offenders. I found relief. Lewis Smede once said, "I let the prisoner go, only to discover the prisoner was me."[xv] Unforgiveness hurts you more than it does the offender.

Let me be clear, forgiveness does not mean you are reconciled to the offender. Forgiveness is a one-way street. Reconciliation goes both ways. Forgiving does not mean you now want to hang out in the hot tub with the offender. It means you refuse to be controlled by your negative feelings. Forgiveness of the offender, even if they never apologize, sets you free.

Living Behind the Collar has been a growth experience in dealing with criticism and learning to forgive. I resolved to be more self-controlled. I discovered a foundation for my life in Christ and His forgiveness of me. Yes, there is a lot of hurt and pain, but blessings and joy are the result of living forgiven and forgiving.

We were fortunate to have limited conflict at both congregations we served. I believe that happened because we were blessed with good, supportive leadership in the church. We also lived in real community with both of these large congregations. They were our family, and families work through conflict and speak the truth in love. Finally, and most importantly, God blessed our bold obedience unto Him and our faith in Him. I discovered I cannot please everyone. I also discovered I didn't need everyone's approval. I found my security in who I am, a child of God, and what He called me to do Behind the Collar.

Chapter 7

I Will Praise You
in This Storm

"It's leukemia!" Those were the words I heard when the doctor called with news of Tristen's bloodwork. I dropped the phone, collapsing into the sofa. My husband picked up the phone, finished the conversation with the doctor, who suggested we get Tristen to the nearest emergency room. My husband explained to him that we were in Houston visiting, but had just moved to Mansfield, and Tristen was at a friend's house playing.

The doctor, sounding relieved, said, "Oh, he can talk to you and smile at you?"

This was a hint as to how bad my son's bloodwork looked.

My husband said again, "Yes, he is playing at a friend's house."

The doctor replied, "I would take him to the hospital closest to where you live. It will be the most convenient place for him to get treatments."

I was so nervous I was trembling. Not knowing what else to do, I started getting his things together to head to the hospital. My mind was racing. *'This can't be happening,'* I thought.

My sister, Donna, picked up our other son, Taylor, so she could take care of him. We jumped in the car, wondering, *"Which hospital do we go to? Houston or Dallas Fort Worth? Which hospital? Which hospital?"*

We had just moved from our home in Houston where we had lived for 20 years to a smaller town named Mansfield in the Dallas/Fort Worth area. After years of working in a large church, my husband had decided to follow the call to a small church. Although I was very close to the members of our church in Houston, I was looking forward to the slower pace of a small church in a small town. Our children were still young. Taylor was in the 4th grade and Tristen was in the 2nd grade. I believed this would be good for my husband and for our family.

It was not an easy decision to make. After my husband received the call to St. John Mansfield, he decided to go off for a weekend and fast and pray. He came home and let me know, God was leading him to take the call. I was committed to following wherever God may lead us, and it looked like He was leading us to Mansfield, Texas.

We still loved our church in Houston. It was very difficult to say goodbye to the people who had been our family for 20 years. We had been through so much with this congregation. Our children were baptized there. They went to school there. Our life centered around that church. Our last Sunday came at this place we called our second home, and my husband preached his last sermon. They had a big party for us and sent us away with their blessings.

The following Sunday, my husband preached his first sermon at our new church in Mansfield. They had a small party to welcome us. The congregation was smaller, and different, but they seemed excited to have us. I already missed our church family in Houston, but I knew this group of excited, friendly people would eventually become our new family.

I enrolled the boys in the public school. They had always gone to the church school affiliated with our church in Houston, so this was a little different. They seemed to adjust quickly. They loved the school and loved that they didn't have to wear a uniform anymore. They made friends. They seemed to like this new place.

While my husband was busy meeting with various groups of people in our new church, I was looking for a home so we could get settled. I had signed our boys up to play league basketball. They loved sports and were natural athletes. I noticed our younger son was struggling to run up and down the court. He had struggled with back pain before we moved from Houston. The pediatrician in Houston checked him out and said he probably just had some stretched muscles.

Tristen was not a complainer, so we had no idea how poorly he was feeling. His stamina seemed to be fading. Since we had moved to Mansfield, I thought I would bring him to a doctor here for another opinion. I asked around and got names of good doctors and made an appointment.

I told the doctor I thought he may have a collapsed lung, since he had some back pain and was quickly winded running down the basketball court. The doctor checked him out, did a chest x-ray and sent us home. He called to let me know the x-ray was clear and everything was fine.

Hmmm, okay. I thought. Then I wondered, "Is my son getting lazy?" It was hard to believe. He had always been so active.

Basketball season ended and baseball season came around. I signed both the boys up. I was unable to be at the first practice, but the coach called to ask me if it was normal for Tristen to tire out after ten minutes of throwing the ball?

I told him no, but I had taken him to see doctors, one in Houston and one here in Mansfield, and they both said he was fine.

He said, "I've coached a lot of boys, and this is not normal. I think he has asthma."

I called the doctor I had taken Tristen to see earlier that week. I told him what the coach had said. He told me to bring him in on Friday, and they would do a full battery of tests.

Tristen hadn't been to a doctor many times in his eight years of life, so this blood draw was a little scary for him. Even so, he was brave, even then. After we left the doctor's office, we went home to get his brother and his dad because we were heading back to Houston for spring break. They were excited to see their old friends. We needed to do a few things to our house, which was on the market.

That Monday morning in Houston, I got the phone call… *'Which hospital do we go too? Which hospital?'*

We started the drive back to the Fort Worth area. A few miles into the trip, we abruptly stopped. What are we doing? Some of the best hospitals in the world are in Houston, Texas. Should we turn around and go back? We paused. We prayed. And then we drove to Cooks Children's Hospital in Fort Worth. I climbed into the backseat of our car so I could sit next to my son. I felt a strong need to be close to him. He, on the other hand, was upset about leaving Houston. He had been looking forward to playing with his old friends. I told him we would drive back to Houston that night if everything checked out.

When we arrived at the hospital, the doctor was waiting for us at the Emergency room. With him was the child life specialist, who was educated and clinically trained in the developmental impact of illness and injury on children. The child life specialist started talking to Tristen, letting him know they were going to draw blood again and re-test.

We waited for what seemed like a long time. The doctor finally came in and asked us to step out to talk privately with him. My insides turned to mush. I knew it was not going to be good news. I was right.

The blood-test confirmed that our 8-year-old son had ALL — Acute Lymphoblastic Leukemia. The protocol for this blood cancer required three years of treatment. The first year would be the hardest. They scheduled Tristen for surgery and his first chemotherapy treatment the next morning. By then, it was already after midnight, and my husband said he would stay the night with our son. He wanted me to go home and rest so I could be there for Tristen in the morning. I went home, only to lay in my bed and wail. Deep inconsolable wailing. I couldn't stop!

Why him, God? Why?

I returned early the next morning for Tristen's surgery. They put a double lumen central line in his chest and gave him his first dose of chemotherapy.

The long journey began.

The news spread like wildfire. We received calls, cards, food, gifts, visits, and comfort from family and friends. Tristen's friends, the ones he had gone to Houston over spring break to play with, came to Fort Worth to see him in the hospital. Everyone wanted to help. The large church family we had left behind in Houston was there for us. The small church family we were just beginning to get to know stepped up to help us as well. Life became a blur, just trying to get through the day… just make it through the hour. One hour at a time, we struggled to get through the day.

Does that make sense? Even as I'm writing this, I feel the desperation all over again. Have you as a parent ever felt that? If so, you know what I'm talking about.

In 2004, the survival rate for ALL was 80 percent, which was encouraging. However, the doctor said his leukemia was "abnormally large" and "hardy." We didn't understand until later what that meant: This leukemia was not normal. It was harder to kill. Still, 8 out of 10 survived. We didn't want to face the fact that 2 out of 10 die.

Tristen completed the first phase of intense chemotherapy called the induction phase. It is designed to put the patient in remission. The bone marrow test revealed the leukemia was being wiped out, but not to the mark they considered remission. The descriptive "hardy" was getting real. The doctors changed his classification to "high risk" and decided to "beef" up the chemo and put him through a second induction phase. I didn't see how he could survive that. The first round had been brutal.

Behind the Collar, we had faced a lot of challenges, but this one knocked me to my knees, literally. I prayed more than I ever had before. We would take three steps forward only to get knocked back two steps. During a meeting with the oncology team, we discussed our options. They were dismal. There was no good answer. After the meeting, we walked out, and my husband said, "We have to start praying harder."

I replied, "Why? It has not done us any good so far!" In my emotional exhaustion, I was losing faith.

I was so angry. How could this happen? Our family had always served God. We had always served the church; served the people. I didn't understand how God could let this happen to his faithful servants. Where was He? Why did this happen? Why hadn't Tristen been healed? Why couldn't he just hit the mark of remission? I couldn't believe it. In my despair, I decided I was done with God. Done!

My doneness lasted all of 24 hours. When I didn't have a God to turn to, to pray to, to place my faith and hope in, I fell deeper into despair. I started praying again. St. Paul said, "Give thanks in all circumstances" (I Thessalonians 5.18). He did not say "give thanks for all circumstances" he said, "in all circumstances." I began to praise Him in the storm. I gave thanks to God for who He is, who He has always been. I still couldn't understand why this was happening. But I was not willing to trade what I knew about God for what I didn't know about Him. I knew He was for me, not against me. He did not cause this leukemia. I asked Him for forgiveness. I asked

Him for strength. I asked for peace in my soul and for wisdom in my mind. I begged Him for Tristen's remission! I discovered God was there. He was with me, He was with my family, and He was with Tristen. Unexpectedly, at the last moment, Tristen went into remission. I gave thanks.

I had always believed remission meant the cancer was gone. That is not what it means. The doctor explained to me, "Remission means the cancer is below the level of detection." So, yes, the induction phases, intended to achieve remission, were over. The next phase was the consolidation phase which still involved rounds of chemo treatment. This phase was tough as well. Tristen had quite a few hospital stays during this phase. Our family began to adjust to this new normal.

At the same time, my husband had taken this new job at this new church in Mansfield. What were we going to do? Our child 's needs obviously came first. My husband spoke to the church leaders, and they agreed to let him decide how to handle the situation, leaving the decision up to him. He juggled the needs of our family and the needs of the church. He was there for our son and for our family while laying the foundation to move the church forward.

Tristen was in the hospital a lot that first year due to the massive amounts of chemo he was taking. We decided I would spend the days at the hospital with Tristen, and my husband would stay the night with Tristen. This worked out because he was working at the church during the day and I was learning about Tristen's medical treatments and how to take care of him when he was able to come home.

He eventually did come home. My challenge was the home health care required. I never thought I would be able to take care of his central line. I could not bear to look at that tube coming out of his chest, but someone had to do it, and that someone was me. Tristen also had a vigorous regimen of medicines. My husband and I worked together to support this effort. An article, Children with Chronic Conditions, stated that, "Divorce is somewhat more common in families with seriously ill children, mainly because of the great stress of parenting an ill child."[xvi] In our case, our relationship was already strong, but it became stronger. We had to communicate precisely. We could not make a mistake in his care. We had another son who, I'm sad to say, had been put on the back burner. His life had been put on hold, but he was relieved to have his brother home and have some normalcy again.

Our new church family was there waiting for us to let them know when and how they could help. Some brought meals. Some would sit with Tristen and Taylor while we went out looking for a home to buy. Others offered to run errands for me. Slowly, we were getting to know our new church family. The same was true here as it had been at our last church: this family of believers loved and supported us.

What I didn't figure on was that this small church would turn into a big job. As I mentioned earlier, my husband Bill had started laying the foundation to move this new church forward. The leadership of the church wanted to act on it. They started making small changes. Sunday morning worship began to change. The church began to grow. There was excitement in the air on Sunday mornings. Ushers were having to pull in chairs to accommodate the new visitors coming in.

The people had outgrown the little chapel, and Easter was coming. We were expecting large crowds for Easter Sunday. My husband told the leadership, "We can take out the walls at the back of the church, or we can tell our visitors to go to hell." For better or for worse, that is a moment for which he will always be remembered. They took out the walls and set up chairs in the back. The church continued to grow.

During this time, our son's health went up and down. It was hard for him, as well as hard for us as his parents. His brother, Taylor, was like a guardian angel to him—most of the time. Tristen was able to start back to school, and I was nervous for him. I did not know how kids would react. His face was swollen, his color ashen, and he had no hair. The school allowed him to wear a do-rag or a cap. Joyfully, thanks to a wonderful third grade teacher named Mrs. Bennett, he was accepted! The kids were so happy to see him back at school. The friends he made in that class became his best friends!

He finished a 3-year treatment plan toward the end of his 4th grade year. The bone marrow test was still showing remission. He would continue to have clinic visits but no more treatment. We were thrilled. I signed him up for baseball, and he got to play. Even though he had missed a few years, you couldn't tell. His coach put him at 3rd base, and he cleaned up everything that was hit around him effortlessly. His brother played in a basketball league. That was his sport. They both played the piano. Things were back to normal. Our church was still growing. I had a wonderful job managing a gift shop at the new hospital near us.

The summer after Tristen's fifth grade year, at one of the clinic visits, his blood test revealed the leukemia was back. He looked at me immediately and started crying and said, "Mom, I'm going to die."

I had to stay strong. I said, "No, Tristen, you can have a bone marrow transplant. Remember, Taylor is a perfect match."

His doctor spoke up and said, "Yes, that's your ace in the hole."

Inside, I knew this was going to be a battle. In order to have a transplant, he would still have to achieve remission. It was hard the first time, it would be even harder this time.

Here we go again, I thought.

Tristen had surgery the next morning. This time they put a port in his chest, and he began his first round of chemotherapy. He was not achieving remission. We signed a consent to use a chemo that was from a St. Jude protocol and had been working well with leukemia. It was strong, and it knocked him down for some time. Then came the moment to take bone marrow and see if this chemo regimen had worked. I was at the hospital with Tristen when they took the bone marrow. I was so nervous about the outcome.

Before the results came back, I had to leave to go to work. I turned to say goodbye to Tristen and glanced at the doctor with an uneasy look.

The doctor said, "Don't worry, it's going to be fine."

As soon as I got off work, I drove back to the hospital. My mom had been there with Tristen during the day. When I got off the elevator, the doctors intercepted me. I knew it wasn't good. They took me to a room and gave me the bad news. Not only did it not work, the leukemia had increased. I rattled off words that I can't write in this book. The doctors looked at me with sympathy.

I asked them, "What happens now?"

They said, "He probably has about two weeks to live. We will make him comfortable."

They also let me know that the head of Oncology was coming back from San Angelo and might have another plan. I was crying. The doctors were crying. I believe they were in disbelief also. This medical team had become part of our family too. They had been through so much with us, and they loved our son. I pulled myself together to go face Tristen.

Tristen knew it wasn't good news because the doctors had been waiting all afternoon to talk to me in person. When he asked me if it worked, I dug deep for strength and told him, "No, it didn't, but Dr. Bowman is headed back from San Angelo and he is coming up with another plan." Which was true. Dr. Bowman was not giving up, and neither were we.

What do you do when you hit rock bottom? You remember that Jesus is the rock. He is our sure foundation. He loves us and died in our place so we could be in His place—heaven. He is for us, not against us. Our prayer life was fervent. We read the promises of God and prayed them. We pleaded before the throne of God for our son. And so did many others.

My husband took Tristen on a short prayer journey. They started at our church in Mansfield. Our church family came together and prayed over Tristen. They left the next morning for Houston. They went to our other church family, St. Mark. A large group prayed over him there. He took Tristen to a place called Serenity where they pray for healing. The last place they stopped was Lakewood Church, and Dodie Osteen came out to the welcome area and prayed over Tristen. Tristen said, "Something is different, I've never felt such love."

Something was different.

The next morning, Tristen and my husband went to clinic for his appointment to run blood tests. The doctor came through the door with a pleasant, but puzzled look on his face. He said, "We can't find any leukemia in Tristen's blood."

My husband said, "That's a miracle."

The doctor said, "Well it is close to a miracle."

The good news was, he was in remission. He was now a candidate for a bone marrow transplant, and his brother was a perfect match.

We faced another long tough battle that involved chemotherapy and radiation. He reached the point where he was ready for the transplant. His brother, Taylor, went into surgery. They took the maximum amount of bone marrow possible from Taylor to give to Tristen.

Tristen was in the bone marrow unit for six weeks, give or take a few days. He pulled through and finally got to come home. His immune system recovery took a while. Slowly but surely, though, our life returned to some kind of normal.

The church continued to move ahead. Our church family in Mansfield had always dreamed of a new building. It happened! We came together as a family and fulfilled the dream God had put into these families' hearts. Under the direction of two very strong businessmen, we formed teams to raise money and build a new worship center, café, gymnasium, bookstore, and classrooms.

Excitement was everywhere! The city of Mansfield had a population of 34,000 in 2004 and had grown to 46,000 by the time we built the church. New people came in, and we grew rapidly. We added more staff and touched the needs of more people.

The boys were excited to be in school. Tristen was in the 7th grade and having the time of his life. He was looking forward to playing basketball. His doctor told him he would need to wait until next year because he was still in recovery. He took it well.

Tristen said he felt better than he had ever felt. Taylor was a freshman in high school, and he was playing basketball. Tristen loved going to watch him play. He really looked up to his brother. He wanted to be like him. We were all enjoying life. Finally, I could exhale. I could relax.

Tristen was expected to go to the oncology clinic once a month for check-ups. In September, 2009, my husband took Tristen for his monthly clinic visit. They did the routine blood test and two doctors walked into the room where my husband and Tristen were. My husband said to them, "Well, tell me the good news." They both looked down. My husband said, "No, no, this can't be."

It was. The leukemia was back.

Tristen was admitted into the hospital for another round of chemo. I was in shock. How could this be? The fight against leukemia began again. We were in September of his eighth-grade year. He had just come off of what he called "the best year of his life." The lead doctor, once again, was trying to come up with another plan. Tristen spent the first several months in the hospital in Fort Worth. He did not go into remission. We were in a race against time. Our last option was to go to St. Jude's Hospital for a trial treatment that included a transplant from one of his parents.

Tristen was in a fight for his life. We were all in a fight for his life.

At times, we didn't know what to pray for. We relied on God's word. The apostle Paul wrote, "In the same way, the spirit helps us in our weakness. We do not know what we ought to pray for, but the spirit himself intercedes for us with groans that words cannot express." (Romans 8.26) Thank God the Spirit knew what to pray in these circumstances! We kept him busy.

While Tristen was in the hospital in Fort Worth, our church family continued to lift us up. During crucial times, many of the Elders would show up to pray for him. He had lots of visitors who brought food, gifts, and encouragement. One sweet family spent their Thanksgiving Day preparing us a complete homemade thanksgiving meal and bringing it to the hospital. My husband, Tristen, Taylor, and I sat around a table in his room and had the most beautiful thanksgiving lunch ever. I will never forget the Shaw family or their kindness.

We finally got the word that St. Jude's Children's Hospital would take us. I was the one who qualified to be the cell donor. We went to St. Jude at the end of January. I underwent a lot of testing. They started Tristen on a vigorous regimen of treatment to get his bone marrow prepared for my cells. Sometime in March, they took my cells and gave them to him. It took weeks to take hold in his marrow, but finally, it did.

All through this book I have said, make your church your family. This is when the reality of those relationships proved to be invaluable. When we couldn't hold on, they held on to us! My husband and I took turns going back and forth to St. Jude Hospital in Memphis, Tennessee. But there came a point where we both needed to be with Tristen. One family took in our other son Taylor to live with them while we were away. Taylor would come visit when we could arrange it. Tristen wanted to see him and would talk to him about things he wouldn't share with us.

Time was precious. We wouldn't leave Tristen alone. We were emotionally and physically exhausted. We needed help. Teams of people from our church family in Houston and from our church family in Mansfield set up a schedule. They would come to Memphis in teams of two and stay, usually for a week. We wanted someone with him at all times. Even at St. Jude's Children's Hospital, mistakes are made.

We were in Tennessee from the end of January until the middle of August. During this time, we had lots of ups and downs. We had miracles. We had hope. Sometime in May, things took a turn for the worse. Tristen ended up in ICU for most of that summer. He made it back to the bone marrow unit of the hospital in August. I really believed we were going to bring him home. We didn't. He died August 14, 2010. The fight was over. When Tristen breathed his last breath on this planet at 5:15 a.m., he breathed his first breath in heaven.

Allow me to pause for a moment. Tears still flow as I remember my son and this difficult journey. My body remembers the numbness. The apostle Paul wrote, "….you do not grieve like the rest of mankind, who have no hope" (1 Thessalonians 4.13). You never get over the loss of a loved one, but it does get better. I also know that God knows what I am going through. His son died on a cross. I believe that when Jesus died on a cross and the Temple four-inch curtain to the holy of holies was split down the middle, it meant that we personally were granted access to the Father. I also believe that it meant that our Heavenly Father was doing what any Jewish father would do when his child died—he tore his clothes. Our heavenly Father knows what it is like to lose a son, but He also knows about resurrections. That is how I grieve, but not as those who have no hope. I know I will see Tristen again. I'm catching my breath now. If you will turn the next page, you will discover more of what happened Behind the Collar.

Chapter 8

Graves to Gardens

We buried him on a hot, windy day in East Texas. His grave was under a tree next to a lake. He would have liked that. I couldn't believe it was over. It was not. I began a forever journey into grief. I felt like they buried two dead people that day—Tristen and me.

After Tristen died at St. Jude, we packed our things and started driving the 8-hour journey home. I was riding with my friend, Becky. My husband and our son Taylor were in a car somewhere behind us. I was numb! I was in a state of shock. It does not matter how long someone has suffered. It does not matter that you knew they might die. It was a loss, a loss unfathomable. My son Tristen was dead. My heart was broken, literally.

While Becky was driving, I was on autopilot. Amid the shock and grief, I got on the phone, called our minister of music, a dear friend, and started planning Tristen's service. When Becky asked, "Where do you want the memorials to go?" the first thing I said was, "A prayer garden." Before anyone purchased flowers, I wanted to let people know we wanted all his memorials to go toward a prayer garden at our church. St. Jude had a beautiful garden where we spent a lot of time. Tristen loved to go there. We finished the call. The service was almost done, and so was I.

Suddenly, a God moment happened. A song came on the radio by Mercy Me. I had never heard it before, and I never heard it again after the Memorial. It was called "Homesick." When I heard it, the tears I had been holding back poured down my cheeks. With a broken voice, I called our minister of music again. I said, "This song has to be sung at Tristen's memorial service."

The song says, "In Christ, there are no goodbyes, and in Christ, there is no end." I knew that in my head, but my heart was struggling with the feeling of finality. I called our minister of music with new ideas. Before I arrived home, we had the memorial service planned. How I could even think surprised me. I believe that God spoke to me during that song and gave me the strength to arrange the service.

We arrived home to a house full of family—biological family, and church family—trays of food and lots of love. Our doorbell did not stop ringing. Someone from church dropped off plasticware, a neighbor brought a beautiful tray of sandwich fixings. One of my friends brought me a sixpack of Shiner Bock. It was good to be home with family and friends. I took a sleep aid early that night and collapsed.

The next few days were more of the same—going through the moments on autopilot. We made arrangements at the funeral home. We visited a floral shop and picked out flowers for his casket. We tied up loose ends for the service. I contacted Tristen's doctor at Cook Children's Hospital in Fort Worth and a few of his coaches. I asked them each to write a blurb about Tristen for the back of the service folder. They all agreed.

I tried to hold my emotions together. What looked strong and brave on the outside was really shock and disbelief on the inside. I was walking around in a paralyzing numbness. My head was in a blur. It was surreal. I felt like I was outside of my body. I could see myself smiling and acting like I was on top of things. I knew that was not true. How do you keep it together when your 15-year-old son dies?

Our church family was busy making sure the church facility could accommodate friends and family coming for the service. They expected over a thousand people. They provided seating for 1300 people by setting up chairs in the sanctuary, the gym, the Sunday school rooms and the gathering area. The tech team set up a livestream so the service could be viewed in all these areas. They recruited young men to park cars out in the field if the parking lot became full.

The praise team met and practiced the music for the service. We had picked a lot of favorites like "I Can Only Imagine," "Homesick," and Third Day's version of "Blessed Assurance." Tristen's elementary school principal played the organ for the opening and closing songs, "How Great Thou Art" and "Amazing Grace." Tristen loved his principal, and the principal loved him. Once, when we had to take Tristen to the ER, I had gone to park my car, and by the time I got to the room where Tristen was, his principal was already there praying for him. Another friend of Tristen's and our family, Barbara, played the trumpet for the opening and closing song. She had been the faithful keeper and updater of all the notes on Care Pages that went out daily during Tristen's battle.

Bill had asked a pastor friend, Dr. Robert Preece, to do the message for the service. Bill knew that Dr. Preece would bring a message of hope and joy in the midst of tragedy.

Spring Creek Bar-b-que said they would do the meal after the service for free. They had that kind of community heart.

I have been describing as best I can the preparation that went into this service. I do not think there was anything left undone. Everyone involved in the service had been touched by Tristen and his story at some point. The musicians who performed had known him personally and had rooted for his recovery. Tristen's doctors and coaches wrote heartfelt blurbs about how Tristen had touched their lives, which were printed in the back of the service folder. This was our church family in our community called Mansfield. They were the ones working behind the scenes to make this happen. We could not have gone through the trauma of losing our son without them. We could not have prepared this amazing service without them, and you will see later in this chapter, they continued to help us through the grieving process following the loss.

The day came for us to publicly say goodbye to our son. I had gone to my husband's office to escape for a moment. His office phone was ringing, and I decided to answer it in case someone needed him. On the other end of the phone was Jerry Kieschnick, the same man who called to check on me when I left my husband. Even though he was now the President of the Lutheran Church Missouri Synod, he was still a pastor to pastors and their families. He was checking on us and let me know he was sorry for our loss, and he and his wife Terry were praying for us. Our church family wasn't just in Mansfield and Houston, it was all over.

People came from Texas, Tennessee, Louisiana, and California to attend. They started arriving early. All the chairs were filled, and those who didn't get a seat stood along the sanctuary walls. I saw friends from our Houston church family, friends of Tristen's along with their parents, friends of Taylor and their parents, teachers, coaches, co-workers, nurses, and administrative staff from Cook Children's Hospital. A nurse from St. Jude and her boyfriend drove over 8 hours to attend. Fellow pastors of our denomination plus other community pastors came. Our biological family, godparents, and of course, our St. John family were there to support us. It was a wonderful service of thanksgiving to God and a tribute to Tristen. For the first time in weeks, I began to smile—a real smile.

The service ended, and we buried his body the next day. We drove the 120-mile trip to the graveside and then back home without saying a word. My smile was fading. The reality was setting in.

Now what was I to do? My home was changed forever. I would sit down for breakfast or dinner at a table that seats four, and it was painfully obvious that the chair where Tristen used to sit was empty. A friend suggested I change the direction of the table or remove the chair. I did. It did not matter; the emptiness was in me and my husband and our son, Taylor. We all walked around like the life had been sucked right out of us. When we began to start rising out of that desperate, defeated state, it wasn't pretty. Anger began to show its ugly face.

I had prayed through Tristen's illness. I had praised God in this storm. We had witnessed miracles all through the journey. We had him with us years longer than we were told we would. I knew God's hand was on him. What I didn't know was, "Why didn't God save him? Why? Why?" I hate to admit it, but I was having bursts of anger! At God! Honestly, everyone in our house was screaming at one time or another, even the pastor. We were not prepared to deal with a loss of this magnitude.

Neither was our church.

My husband came home from a meeting one night. He looked at me with disbelief and said, "For some reason or another, I can't seem to get our people motivated." It occurred to me that they were still grieving this loss. They had walked through the fire with us, and they had not recovered either. One of the elders let him know just that. He said, "We went through this with you. We were part of your family, and we mourn deeply also."

This family of believers had been with us through the six-year journey of Tristen's illness. Tristen's struggle was St. John's struggle. In the article, "A Look Inside Family Life When Someone is Dying," it states, "Family is oftentimes defined by people based on various kinds of bonds, emotional ties, and the qualities of the relationship between people."[xvii] Our church family fit that statement. We had bonded through this journey. They had felt the desperation we were feeling that year, and I believe they felt like they had the life sucked out of them too.

I think they looked to my husband and me to see how we were responding. They didn't know how to mourn with us. How do you grieve when the pastor's son dies? The pastor is the strong one. He is usually the one they could turn to for comfort. We were all dying on the inside, and we didn't know who to turn to. In the midst of this grief, we were fortunate to have a young associate pastor, Pastor Danny, who helped keep the congregation together.

We all process grief differently. I had to be busy, which was my way of avoiding the inevitable grieving. I would be doing something, and then in my "down" time, I would burst into tears. My grieving may have taken longer, although I don't think there is a specific length of time appropriate when you're grieving the loss of your child. It is a lifelong journey. I can say, eventually, the good days came to outnumber the bad days.

During one of my outbursts, I asked my husband, "Who is the person in the district whose job it is to help pastors and their families when they are in need?" At church, I was acting like my old self. I walked around with a smile, greeting people and loving on people. On the inside, I was broken. I felt like part of me had died. I struggled with when, where, and how do I get this brokenness put back together? Even at home, I wanted to be strong for Taylor, our other son. The loss of Tristen had undoubtedly altered his life. They were close in age and remarkably close to each other. He didn't just lose his brother. He lost sane parents. We were mentally struggling. My husband was always the rock, but I knew he was broken too.

Bill called a friend who is a pastor and counselor to church workers in the Pacific Southwest District of the Lutheran Church, Missouri Synod. He asked him if he could spend some time with me. His name was Ron Rehrer. He was on a plane to Texas within a couple of days. Ron and I sat in my living room and visited. We talked about Tristen and this long journey. I described to him this unimaginable void I had deep in my core. When you lose your child, you lose the future, too—the graduation from high school and college, their career. Tristen wanted to be a doctor or a pastor. Probably because most of his life was spent around doctors and pastors. There would not be a wedding or grandchildren. I began to cry. I cried and cried. He encouraged me to just let go. He let me know emotional release was important, and he gave me permission to let it out. It was helpful. I was able to empty some of the heaviness I had been carrying around. I was reminded, not only was it okay to ask for help, it was good to ask for help.

I made appointments with another counselor for our son, Taylor. I realized, being able to talk and cry and yell if you need to was cleansing. I believed that helped him too. We were all learning to live with a "new normal."

Slowly, but surely, we moved through the process of grief. Elizabeth Kubler Ross, in her book, "Death and Dying," describes the grief cycle as 5 stages. Denial, anger, bargaining, depression, and acceptance.[xviii] For me, the 5 stages of grief were not linear but cyclical. I would go from acceptance to depression frequently.

One of the blessings, that was therapy for me, was to participate in the design and building of the prayer garden. There were very few flowers at his memorial service, but many memorials to go to the prayer garden. I knew the flowers at the service would eventually die and be gone, but the flowers in the garden would continue to live. I thank our church family for allowing us to do that and to have a large piece of property that was in a significant location. You know what they say; location, location, location! We built the garden in front of the chapel and it was easily seen by cars on the most traveled street in Mansfield. Before the garden, there was nothing there except a large square of grassy land.

I worked with a landscape designer. She was well known for great designs. The first part built was the water feature. It was a waterfall that consisted of large rocks and small rocks. Tristen's brother, Taylor, planted the first two trees. They were oaks. We also had three little gem magnolias, three crepe myrtles, and one Chinese pistachio. The flowers in the garden consisted of azaleas, knockout roses, and seasonal plantings. It was and still is absolutely beautiful.

The garden has become an asset to the church. Every day, people go out there for quiet time and prayer. Preschool classes release butterflies in it every year. Graduation pictures, wedding pictures, family pictures, all kinds of moments are captured in the garden. It has even served as a place for small weddings, vow renewals, and even baptisms. My husband has baptized several in the waterfall. A homeless man would come and sleep on the grass. He loved the garden. We helped him out with clothes, shoes, and a motel to sleep, although he preferred the garden. We were able to witness to him. The garden eventually became a place of remembrance and life.

Sitting there during the day, my thoughts steadily wandered from graves to gardens.

Jesus, according to the Apostle John, was buried in a grave, a tomb located in a garden. (John 19.41) That grave on Easter Sunday was empty. The message of Christianity is confirmed by the empty tomb. The good news that Jesus conquered death for all His followers was to me, a message from graves to gardens. I held on to hope that in Jesus, my son was more alive than ever because of that grave in the garden. As I thought about this, I suddenly realized that Jesus was bringing me out of my grave of despair and brokenness and into the garden of hope.

I made a choice to be better. Our church hosted Don Piper, author of "90 Minutes in Heaven" as a guest speaker. I told him we had lost our son. He let me know, "No, ma'am, you didn't lose your son, you know right where he is, and I'm sorry for your temporary separation, but that's what it is. You're going to see him again." His message that evening was, you can be bitter, or you can be better. He was right. I had a choice and I chose to be better. I'm not saying there weren't days that I would be bitter, but many more days I was better. You, too, must make that choice when bad things happen. You can get bitter, or you can get better.

I found continued love and encouragement from my church family. I also found work. I had lost my job during our long stay at

St. Jude. It was important for me to be active and have purpose. I was able to stay plenty busy at our church as a part-time employee.

Another important factor in my healing was exercise. My emotions, at first, were up and down. I was grasping at any and everything I could to feel better. At times, I didn't think this feeling of despair that lay just under my skin was ever going to leave. When I went to the doctor for my yearly checkup, the doctor asked me how I was doing. I smiled and said, "Fine." Then I burst into tears. He said he could give me something that would just take the edge off until I could get through this sadness. I told him no, but that I would start exercising, and I knew that would help.

So, I started to exercise, and it did! Fortunately for me, my first day in the gym, I met an instructor named Elly, who I loved. She was tough, but she was motivating and inspiring. She cared. She really didn't know who I was. She just cared. She cared for everyone and inspired them to work hard and do their best as well. I went back day after day for that 5 am class. I didn't want to miss it. It helped me get physically and mentally stronger. I credit Elly and that class as one of the things that healed my brokenness.

Allow me to be very clear. Everyone grieves differently. Those were just some of the things I did to begin to heal. Once I quit bouncing back and forth between the stages of grief, I finally came to acceptance. I started focusing on how Tristen lived instead of how he died. I became thankful for the years we had Tristen, and I treasured those memories. It took years, but I stepped out of that grave and started to live again.

David Kessler, an associate working with Elizabeth Kubler Ross before she died, gained permission from her to add a 6th stage of grief. He wrote a book called Finding Meaning: The 6th Stage of Grief. In his book, he states that mourning becomes different, and people can heal faster when they find meaning in the memory of the loss of their loved one. He pointed out that Walsh found meaning after his son was murdered by creating America's Most Wanted. The mother whose daughter was killed by a drunk driver started MADD — Mothers Against Drunk Drivers.[xix]

How did we find meaning? We looked at the core of Tristen's life, which was love and service for others.

We were thankful to have the "Tristen Dasch Prayer Garden" and all the beautiful purposes it serves. We also wanted to do things on his birthday or Christmas that honored him and gave meaning to his life and the things he loved.

In his memory, we gave Cook Children's Hospital a large blanket warmer. It was Tristen's idea and Tristen's money.

During our time at St. Jude hospital, Tristen could get warm blankets anytime he wanted one. They had blanket warmers on every floor. The first thing he said was, "Mom, we have to get Cook's one of these."

The last birthday Tristen was able to celebrate was his 15th. He was in ICU at St. Jude, and somehow word got out that if everyone sent him a dollar, he would have a great birthday. Cards upon cards were delivered to St. Jude for Tristen. Whoever was on shift, sitting with him, would open the cards to read to him, and a one-dollar bill would fall out. We were still opening cards in August when he died.

A few months later, when I could bring myself to finish opening the boxes of unopened cards, I brought the box in and sat on the living room floor. One by one, I opened the cards. A one-dollar bill would drop out. I would read the card, cry, and set the dollar bill aside. The one-dollar bills added up to be a little less than six thousand dollars. I called one of his favorite child life specialists at Cook Children's Hospital to find out how much the blanket warmers cost. Believe it or not, it was a little less than six thousand dollars.

I drove to Cook's the next day. I walked into the Oncology Clinic as I had done so many times before. I gave and received lots of hugs. I also gave them a check for the blanket warmer. I told them this was Tristen's idea and it was Tristen's money. The nurse said, "We will call them Tristen's blankets."

I won't go through year by year, but I do want to share a couple of birthday gifts in honor of Tristen's birthday. The first year after his loss, he would have turned 16. He was known for the buttermilk pie he made. He made it from a recipe of my mom's. His secret was less sugar and always use the real Mexican vanilla. We made four of his buttermilk pies and took them to Cook's Hospital to share with his family of doctors and nurses. You can find the recipe in the appendix.

On his 17th birthday, we sent seventeen dollars to seventeen of his friends to do something helpful for someone. We gave scholarships for college to kids who graduated the year he would have graduated. Every year it has something to do with Tristen and/or to help someone in need. He loved serving and helping others.

The sixth stage of grief, finding meaning, really blessed me. I didn't want people to forget Tristen. I wanted something good to come out of the terrible loss of his life. I still want to feel good about finding meaning in his life even now.

Stepping out of the grave and into the garden required the love of family and an understanding of God. It wasn't easy to find meaning in tragedy, but I found renewed hope once I did. The hope of heaven and the promise of eternal life continues to give me strength. I know that the Lord will bring me to my eternal home one day, where I will see my son again.

I am thankful for how God continues to bless me. 2 Corinthians 4. 16-18 says, "Therefore we do not lose heart. Though outwardly we are wasting away, yet inwardly we are being renewed day by day. [17] For our light and momentary troubles are achieving for us an eternal glory that far outweighs them all. [18] So we fix our eyes not on what is seen, but on what is unseen, since what is seen is temporary, but what is unseen is eternal."

I hope this scripture speaks to you the way it speaks to me; as a potent reminder that no matter what you're going through, Jesus has the power to turn graves into gardens, and hope can be found Behind the Collar.

Chapter 9

I Hope You Dance

The last thing I felt like doing when my husband retired, was dancing. I thought, "I don't like this, I will sit this one out." I didn't know it yet, but I wouldn't sit very long. Dancing would come again.

I finally was getting good at living Behind the Collar when my husband, Bill, retired—well, not retired in the normal sense of the word. Retirement was not about trips to Colorado or cruises to Mexico. It was about a different line of work.

I said to my husband, "I thought you were retiring." He responded, "No, I am refiring." And that's what he did.

Bill decided to end his full-time pastoral ministry after 42 years as a pastor of a Lutheran Church. He immediately began a full-time ministry with the vision of helping the Lutheran Church become a church that prayed for healing and wholeness.

Eleven years earlier, he had gone on a personal retreat to fast and pray about moving from Houston, Texas to Mansfield, Texas. He felt God clearly told him to move to Mansfield and pastor the church there for a time. Then he felt called to move into an intentional prayer ministry that would glorify God through prayer for healing and wholeness. That's what he did!

I was thrilled for my husband. He had worked hard and faithfully served three churches in his forty-two years as a full-time pastor. God had blessed each church with growth, and my husband's work changed many lives. Now he was moving into a new area of ministry. It was his dream, and he was passionate about this new ministry. I said, "I am so excited for you." My excitement quickly faded when I realized I would have to leave my church job and my church home too! Many Lutheran churches suggest a time of separation when a pastor leaves a church. That means his wife must also leave.

I protested, "What do you mean? I am expected to leave because you are leaving?" My church was not just my job. It was my passion, my social circle; it was my family. Now, because my husband wanted to retire and move into his next calling in prayer ministry, I would have to move as well. My heart was with these people I called my church family. We were bonded together. I had invested so much time and energy in this church.

I had always volunteered in the church and would fill in if someone was out, but I worked there for the last several years of his ministry. I did a little bit of everything, from worship planning, assimilation, event planning, hospitality, whatever the staff needed me to do. The staff jokingly called me the "Senior" senior pastor. Not that I was senior in age, but I knew my way around the church. I understood the direction of the church and where we were going. I was connected, and I knew how to connect with other people. I found meaning in my job. I loved serving God alongside the staff.

Now, I didn't know what I was going to do. So, I prayed, "Lord, what do I do now?" I was confused and hurt. Questions plagued me. Where do we serve? Where do we go to church? Can we attend events? Funerals? Weddings? Where are the guidelines for retiring pastors and their families? It felt like the end.

We had researched whether retired pastors could remain a member of the church they had served. There were good reasons for the pastor to move on and good reasons for the pastor to stay. It depended on the individual and the circumstances. We also called district officials within our denomination to find out what they recommended. Our denomination does not have set rules on whether a retired pastor can continue to attend the church he was serving. The district official we spoke with told us, "It depends on the individual and if they were asked to retire or were they planning to retire." They would not want the retired pastor to make trouble for the new pastor — that made sense.

I knew that wouldn't be an issue for us. My husband had decided to retire. He announced his retirement two years early so the church would have plenty of time to plan for his replacement. No one wanted him to retire (well, maybe a couple of people). They also knew he was retiring to start the new ministry to which God had called him. Anyone who knew my husband knew he would support the new pastor.

The church honored my husband with an amazing retirement dinner event called "Decades of Dasch," where the leadership rewarded him for his faithful service. It was a beautiful evening with family and friends surrounding us.

The day after the retirement dinner, Bill finished packing up his office at church and moved into another office downtown to start the prayer ministry. He had already done the foundational work to create this 501c3 ministry (did I mention he loved his work?). I helped him get his office set up and anything else I could do. I did not quite have the vision to understand precisely what this ministry would look like. I usually did not see what he saw. Despite that, I would always stand with him and support him. Like most everything for which he had a vision and a calling, it came true.

As for attending the church from which you retire, we separated for a time. We did not attend our church for the first six months after retirement. We had a great time visiting other churches. On our first Sunday after retirement, we were up and dressed early, like we had done so many Sundays over the years. We decided to get in the car and head to Creekwood Church. My husband was friends with the Minister of Music there. They were competitors on the racquetball court. We were used to being at church by 7:00 a.m. for the 8:00 service. We arrived at 8:15 a.m. for the 9:00 service. To our surprise, Creekwood attendees were late risers, and nobody showed up before 8:45. We were at church too early. Old habits die hard. We laughed. This was going to take some getting used to.

Honestly, it took time for me to adjust to this new season. I went from one hundred to zero. I went from serving to not serving, from purpose to purposeless. My husband still got up and went to work. He was making a difference. I got up each day and didn't know what to do. I have to admit; sometimes, I cried—a lot. I struggled with what to do with my life now. I had just figured out all this Behind the Collar stuff, and suddenly it was gone. Now my work, my family, my purpose, my significance had been taken from me. Thank God I still had my circle of friends, which helped make this season bearable. I knew I was expected to separate from our church family, but I had mixed emotions about that. I deeply missed my church and felt a profound void.

In this season of separation and grief, I learned again that God is great at resurrections. He brought me a new life. I walked through the valley and found his sustaining presence. Even when things did not make sense, I clung to the God who had told Abraham to go to a land to which he had never been before and then made him the father of many nations. I remembered that when God closes one door, he always opens another.

I made the decision not to sit out any longer. I began to dance again.

A new senior pastor arrived six months after my husband retired. I was invited to help plan the welcome service for him and his family. I did, and a spark lit in my head. It was an exciting time. Bill and I let him know right away that he was "our pastor." We were there to support and encourage him. I suppose if he had been insecure or threatened by my husband's presence, it would not have worked, but he was not threatened.

On the contrary, he said, "Why wouldn't I draw from his wealth of experience and wisdom?" He assured us that we were always welcome to attend our home church. He seemed to have a healthy view of the real reason we were all there—to glorify God and work for His kingdom. He invited us to use our gifts as we saw fit in serving God at the church.

My husband and I both have a healthy relationship with the new pastor and his wife. We pray daily for him and his family. Bill and I know that being the lead pastor is a tough job. We know the challenges of leadership. The new pastor, Jon Thomas, has done a wonderful job leading the church. He continued to build on the prayer foundation that had been laid and added more missional ministry. He called on me to help with different projects at the church. I did, gladly. I felt more at peace.

My husband understands boundaries and would never meddle in the politics of the church. He did a few funerals with the permission and blessing of the new pastor. He always lets people know he is not a pastor at the church anymore, and they have three fine pastors to call on. When asked, "What do you think of... at the church," he always politely responds, "I don't."

Although we have the senior pastor's blessing to attend our church home, unfortunately, we rarely do. The healing and wholeness prayer ministry that Bill started keeps us away most weekends. My husband travels to different churches across the United States, teaching and preaching on prayer, healing, and wholeness. I go with him when he drives but not when he flies. I do not like to fly. At times, He also does pulpit supply for churches that are without a pastor. Often, I feel that I have connected to people in these churches. Now I have many churches that I call 'family.'

We were blessed— this was not the end. It was the beginning of new opportunities. T.D. Jakes once said, "Did you not recognize opportunity because it was dressed as adversity?" I did not. It was dressed as a loss. I was looking at the loss of my church, job, and friends instead of the new doors God was opening.

When people ask me, "How is retirement?" I now respond, "I'm having a ball, but Bill is working harder than ever." It is true. God has blessed the healing and wholeness ministry he leads. It is different than running a large church. The stress level in our house has dropped. He does go to the office daily and travels many weekends, but he loves teaching and praying with and for people. He has a passion for helping people and churches discover the gift of God's love and healing in their body, mind, and spirit.

When asked how long he plans on doing this ministry, he responds, "There is no retirement in the bible. Some of God's greatest men were over 75 when they started." That is also true of you. While you may have different interests at different ages or different seasons of your life, the only retirement age in the bible is when you go to heaven. Both Bill and I plan on serving God with the Holy Spirit's help until we die.

No matter the circumstance you may be in or what stage of life you are in, God still wants to use you. He loves you and is with you during the good times and the bad. Adversity often brings opportunity. We continue to serve, whether in our church home or leading conferences at other churches or helping with pulpit supply. We also call on pastors and their wives who may need encouragement.

So, if you are reading this and are thinking, "I'm not retirement age, but I feel discouraged, burnt out, worn out," then maybe you need to "refire." Perhaps God is leading you to a new season. Perhaps, like the Hebrew people, you feel like you have been in the desert for forty years and are dried up. Maybe you need to cross the Jordan into the promised land now. You can choose to sit this one out, or you can choose to dance. That is what the church is about. The church is the body of Christ and is here to love, accept, encourage, and help you find hope. God often works through His people. He put people around you who can help you find renewal and strength. Through the indwelling Holy Spirit, He also gives you living water to revive dry lives to get back into the dance.

During the time of separation from our church, I felt loss and grief. But God gave me a new beginning. I slowly adjusted and found my sweet spot—serving God by serving people. Bill knew his sweet spot from years of ministry—he loves to teach and help people pray for healing. His transition time was minimal. My transition required God's divine intervention to lead me through the valley to His heart. I discovered more of who I am and why I do things. I found I had more time to mentor other pastor's wives. One of my best friends is also a pastor's wife. She had always helped me with events at church. Now, she oversees church events, and I help her when she needs me. I believe she sees me as her mentor. I am not sure who is mentoring who anymore. I love watching others grow Behind the Collar.

As for Bill and I, we are having the time of our lives. All our past experiences have grown us into the people we are today. I recently asked Bill what he thought of what he has observed of me Behind the Collar. Here is what he said:

I married you because I saw the inner person — who you are. You were not only beautiful on the outside; you were beautiful on the inside. You were different than most women. You were excited about life and people. You took risks and were not afraid to fail. I saw your faith in God and knew you were the woman I wanted to marry and grow old with.

During our years together, your excitement about life has only grown. You have a great relationship with God and love to help people. Everyone loves you because they see what I see — a transparent, real, hopeful woman of God.

You don't give up, and you don't give in. You just give to help others. You have taught me about laughter, love, and commitment. I cannot imagine going through all we have been through with anyone else. You have made this life fun and challenging. I thank God for you. With you, I am having the best time of my life.

Our marriage gets better each year. Our faith is growing. I am experiencing life as never before.

Let me tell you about some of my recent joys. I went on a "girls" cruise with friends this past year to Mexico. I am planning a trip to Switzerland with my sister (I'll need sedation for the plane ride). I often travel to see our son Taylor who lives two hours away. I meet weekly with a group of women for wine and talk. I regularly send out cards to people who are experiencing grief. And of course, I have begun to write books.

What I originally saw as a negative—leaving my church—God turned into a positive. He opened new doors of ministry, service, and life. The apostle Paul wrote, "And we know that in all things God works for the good of those who love him, who have been called according to his purpose." (Romans 8.28)

Whether you are young or not so young—your Savior is for you, not against you. The apostle Paul also wrote "I can do all things through Jesus Christ who strengthens me." Here's a quick Sheila Dasch paraphrase of that scripture, "Hang in there. In Jesus, you can make it." God is present, and He has not forsaken you. And yes, there are many good times and blessings on the journey. The reality is that no matter the circumstances, no matter the disappointments, no matter the life changes, you can choose to dance or sit this one out. I hope you dance.

Chapter 10

We've Only
Just Begun

This book has been a snapshot of my journey Behind the Collar. I have learned it, I have lived it, and I have loved it. It has been an honor and a privilege to serve alongside my husband. Yes, there were challenges along the way, but there has been overflowing joy too. I feel blessed beyond measure. I have seen God show up and show out. I have served and been served by two amazing congregations that I love and consider my family. God has blessed me with circles within circles of friends. This is not the whole story, and it is not the end. The journey continues. Your journey will also continue. My prayer is that you have learned from my excursion things that will help you in yours. I hope this book will shorten your learning curve. I have been as transparent as possible, showing you my weaknesses and my strengths. Most of all, I hope you have seen God's hand in my life. The road I traveled has been twisted at times, but it has always led back to a good, good Father who, in baptism, adopted me and calls me His own.

This good Father taught me ten things I want to leave you with as a summary of this book's chapters. Whether you are a wife of a pastor, church member, pastor, or a curious reader, I hope the knowledge I gleaned on my journey helps you on yours. Here are 10 things I want to share with you that God taught me along the way.

1. Only Jesus walks on water. We are all imperfect despite our expectations of perfection in other people or ourselves. The bible is clear on this. "All have sinned and fall short of the glory of God." (Romans 3.23) We are all in the same boat, and if it weren't for Jesus, it would be sinking. So, how did I learn to deal with imperfections in myself and others?

   I learned that God accepts me unconditionally. He loves me just as I am, though He will transform me into a better person than I ever imagined I could be. Guess what? He's doing the same thing with you and all the imperfect people around you. There is no one, I repeat no one, perfect… except for God. God made you unique. He made you in His image. I had to stop trying to remake people based on my own image—what I thought they should be and how they should behave. I gave up the "should" and learned to love people just as they are. Some like to squeeze the toothpaste in the middle, and others roll it up neatly. Either way, it doesn't matter. We are all different. We need to quit trying to change people.

   I urge you to cherish the gift of who you are and appreciate who others are. God has made each of us unique individuals.

The Apostle Paul wrote, "We have different gifts, according to the grace given to each of us" (Romans 12.6). You are one of a kind. No one's fingerprints are like yours. You have a unique identity and destiny. Even though you may be a pastor's wife, I urge you to serve in your area of giftedness, not in the area of people's expectations. Maybe you don't play the piano, but you can play softball. Whatever you do, do it to the glory of God.

2. Loneliness is a curse of our existence. We are separate yet together. You can victimize yourself inadvertently by doing nothing about your situation when you are lonely. You can also refuse to be a victim by reaching out to other people and building relationships. Sometimes, we all need a little help from our friends.

3. As for Pk's, I wasn't the virgin Mary, and my first child was not named Jesus. I was an ordinary mother who had ordinary children. Mine "peed on the ants" in front of the church. I learned to let my kids be kids. They already had pressures from the expectations of the congregation. They didn't need them from me as well. Let them discover who they are in Christ and use their gifts in church just like anybody else.

4. This one burst my Cinderella dream. I learned that marriage is not always a bed of roses, and sometimes the glass slipper doesn't fit my foot. Over the years, my husband and I have said things to each other that we wish we had never spoken.

Someone once said, "You always hurt the one you love." I have done that. And perhaps you have too. I have learned that my pride has often stood in the way of asking forgiveness from the ones I love, but when I got past it and did, it was always worth it.

I learned the importance of prioritizing family. I want to live happily ever after. And my family is my top priority after Jesus. I have learned that I am a better spouse when I surrender myself to Jesus and receive his love and peace and forgiveness. When I do that, I've discovered that I can give more. Someone said, "When a well runs dry, it can't give water." You can't give what you don't have, and if you're empty, you have nothing. But our God is a giving God, and He fills us up every day. "...for his compassions never fail. They are new every morning" (Lamentations 3.22-23). Marriages still work throughout any person's journey. But it is a labor of love. Your communication with each other helps build a strong foundation for your marriage.

Prayer calls down the resources of heaven as you and your spouse pray together. It is difficult to be mad at someone when you are holding their hand and praying for them. God urges us to pray when he says, "Call on me in the day of trouble and I will deliver you" (Psalm 50.15). When you pray together, your relationship has a 99% chance of making it. The divorce rate among couples who go to church regularly is 1 out of 2, the same as unbelievers. According to the Gallop Poll, the divorce rate of couples who pray together daily is 1 out of 1,153.[xx] That's why you see plaques in stores that say, "The family that prays together, stays together."

If you are ever thinking should I stay or should I go? Talk to your spouse. Get help from a professional counselor. Work at making your marriage the best it can be. Together, you and your spouse can rediscover the original joy in your marriage and live "happily ever after."

5. If you're in leadership, you will face criticism. While some criticism may be warranted, there are plenty of times when it is not. Keep in mind *who* is criticizing. It may be someone who is just cruel. It may be someone who doesn't have all the information or know the whole story. When others criticize your spouse in conversation with you, be open and politely let them know, "You need to speak to my husband about the criticism, not me." As you grow, learn to handle criticism about yourself or your family without becoming critical yourself. Whose voice matters to you—God's or man's? The apostle Paul wrote, "I care very little if I am judged by you or by any human court; indeed, I do not even judge myself" (I Corinthians 4.3). These are words to remember when people criticize you or your spouse.

6. Your journey, like mine, will involve suffering and hard times. Being the wife of a pastor does not mean your life will

be a walk in the park with champagne under an old oak tree every day. The devil will attack you because you are making a difference. If you're under attack, you're on the right track. You are manifesting the kingdom of God as you live through the hard times and still lift Jesus high. Christians aren't exempt from suffering, but we have a God who is with us in the midst of our trials. You are never alone. Let His presence bring you peace, hope and strength.

7. God is the only one who can turn graves into gardens. In my journey and yours, illnesses and death will happen to us and or our loved ones. I grieved deeply and lost hope for a while when my son died. You may be nodding in agreement if you have suffered a loss in your life. God restored my spirit when I found eternal hope in my savior who conquered sin, death, and the devil. I have taken comfort in Jesus who rose from the dead and declared, "I am the Living One; I was dead, and now look, I am alive forever and ever! And I hold the keys of death and Hades" (Revelation 1.18). In the midst of the graveyard, I found a garden of hope in Christ. The Psalmist wrote, "You have turned my wailing into dancing" (Psalm 34.11). The you in that verse is Jesus. He is the only one who can turn wailing into dancing and sorrow into joy. No matter the storm, loss of a loved one, loss of a relationship, or severe illness, Jesus is the only one who can turn graves into gardens.

8. When your husband retires, you may be thinking it's over. What's my purpose now? I have learned that what's to come can be better than what has been. There is no such thing as retirement age in the bible. Look at Moses; he was eighty when he got started. Maybe you've never learned how to dance. Perhaps it's time to dance into a new season with gifts and talents in a similar ministry or a new ministry. You still have so much wisdom and vigor to give to the kingdom of God.

   When I was asked what are the three foundational things that have helped me become the woman I am today. I answered, "It really is about relationships—my relationship with God, my relationship and faith in Jesus Christ through the word and prayer, and relationships with my church family."

9. Seasons come, and seasons go. Nothing ever remains the same. We will face many changes during our journeys. There will be good times and bad times. An old fable puts it this way:

   There was a man who had four sons. He wanted his sons to learn to not judge things too quickly. So, he sent them each on a quest, in turn, to go and look at a pear tree that was a great distance away. The first son went in winter, the second in spring, the third in summer, and the youngest son in fall.

   When they had all gone and come back, he called them together to describe what they had seen. The first son said that the tree was ugly, bent, and twisted. The second son said no— it was covered with green buds and full of promise. The third son disagreed. He said it was laden with blossoms that smelled so sweet and looked so beautiful that it was the most graceful thing he had ever seen. The last son disagreed with all of them; he said it was ripe and drooping with fruit, full of life and fulfillment.

The man then explained to his sons that they were all right because they had each seen but one season in the tree's life. He told them that you cannot judge a tree, or a person, by only one season and that the essence of who they are—and the pleasure, joy, and love that come from their lives—can only be measured at the end when all the seasons have come to pass.

If you give up when it's winter, you will miss the promise of your spring, the beauty of your summer, the fulfillment of your fall. Don't let the pain of one season destroy the joy of all the rest.[xxi]

Here's the lesson. How you see the seasons of your life depends on how you think about each season. The bible says, *"for as he thinks within himself, so he is"* (Proverbs 23.7). Your thoughts during a season will determine your feelings, which will influence your actions. I have struggled with the seasons of my journey and how I see them. More and more, I am beginning to understand that I can choose to interpret what I see by what I tell myself about the situation. You can too. It's all in how you look at it.

I want to remind you of God's word in 2 Corinthians 4.16-18, this is the bible verse I go to, no matter the season, "Therefore we do not lose heart. Though outwardly we are wasting away, yet inwardly we are being renewed day by day. For our light and momentary troubles are achieving for us an eternal glory that far outweighs them all. So, we fix our eyes not on what is seen, but on what is unseen, since what is seen is temporary, but what is unseen is eternal." Look at temporary things from an eternal perspective. I like what one person said, "Don't sweat the small stuff. Anything you can't see from 25,000 feet in the air is small stuff." Perhaps you and I need to learn; it's all small stuff.

10. Don't stop the journey. Live until you die. Don't die while you are still alive. Don't give up. There are challenges and joys Behind the Collar. There are seasons that come and go. I journeyed from the illusion of false expectations to the reality of who I am and who my Father is. My own journey took many twists and turns, but God straightened my path and led me to joy and fulfillment. He can do it for you too, Behind the Collar.

My prayer is that you take the lessons from this journey and embrace them. I'd like to pray for you now.

Father God, you alone are worthy of praise and honor and glory. Today, I join with those who are reading this book and worship you.

You are holy, holy, holy. You have created all things, and you have loved and forgiven us in Jesus Christ, our Lord, and Savior. Today, I ask you to release from heaven whatever the person reading this book needs. If that someone is a pastor's wife, I ask that you release more of your love and joy and wisdom upon them. If that person is a church member, I ask you to release love and understanding and support for those Behind the Collar. If that someone is a pastor, I ask you to release love, acceptance, and encouragement for their spouse. I thank you for helping me grow over the years. I ask you to bless all these other people who will walk this path. May we all be driven by your Holy Spirit to join together and help bring in your Kingdom. May lives be changed and relationships be restored as Jesus is lifted high.

You alone are our God, and we love serving you. Hold us all close through your Holy Spirit and Your Word and help us glorify you— Behind the Collar. In the name of Jesus.

Amen

Photos

Oh no, he can't be a pastor.

Oh yea, he's a pastor.

Hunting...the things we do for love.

Pastors' wives make great friends.

Picnic with one of my circle of wow friends.

Dinner with friends.

Pajama party with circle of close friends.

Picnic with my circle of work friends.

Did I mention, I love a good picnic?

Pastors' wives make great friends.

Wonderful friends.

Taylor and Tristen (PK's) in Houston.

Our first born, Taylor.

Taylor and Tristen in Mansfield.

St. Mark Houston Church Directory Photo.

My Grandmother (Mimi) and I.

The boys and I.

Bill and I at St. Mark in Houston.

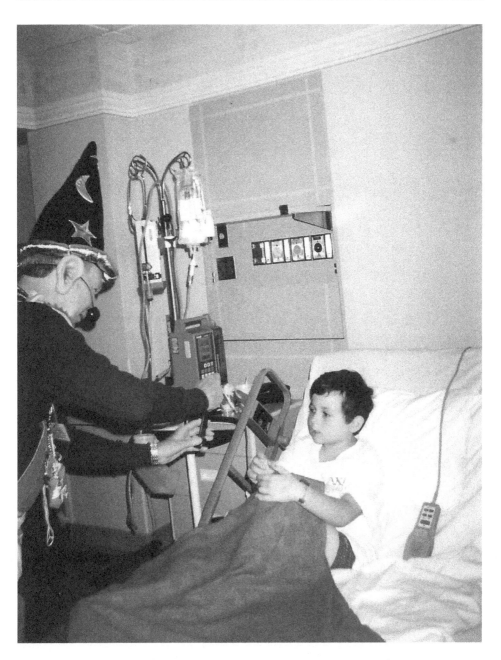

Tristen (2nd grade) first week in hospital.

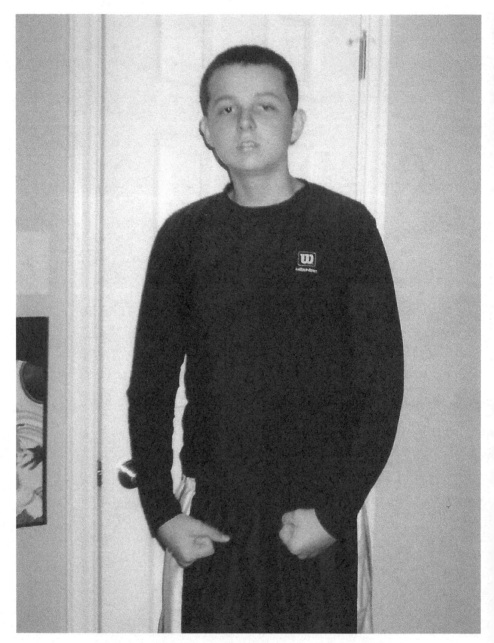

**Tristen (8th grade) the day before we
found out leukemia was back.**

Tristen (6th grade) in the hospital for a bone marrow transplant.

Tristen and I treasuring the moment.

**Tristen (7th grade) in Canada during the
"Best year of his life".**

**Tristen and St. Jude Chef making
buttermilk pie.**

Tristen Dasch Prayer Garden

Tristen Dasch Prayer Garden

Speaking at the Ladies Bluebonnet Luncheon.

Appendix

Handling Criticism

Listening to the Critic to Understand

Step #1 – Listen Without Interrupting

- Repeat back word for word what you hear.
- *"If I'm hearing you correctly, you have a problem with my driving and texting. Is that correct?"* Is there more?

Step #2 – Validate

- That makes sense because.....(give reasons that make sense....If none of this makes sense, ask for more clarification)
- *"That makes sense because I often text while I'm driving and I am not paying attention to the road."*

Step #3 – Show Empathy

"I can imagine when I drive and text you feel (mad, sad, anxious, scared, etc.)" Don't worry about getting the exact feeling right. Most people will correct you if you are wrong. *"No, I don't feel anxious, I feel angry."*

This model of listening shows you're not thinking of what you are going to say next and shows the person who has a problem and is criticizing you or your family that you're really listening to them. This process often solves issues immediately.

Forgiveness Exercise

Sitting down, put your hands on your knees. Imagine your hands holding all the hurts a person has put on you. Visualize the person who has hurt you and say out-loud, "I forgive you." Turn your hands upside down and let all those hurts go. Ask God to cleanse your heart and mind as you end the unforgiveness. When negative ideas or thoughts of hurt return, resist them saying, "In Jesus' power, it is finished." Then go on praising God. Your forgiveness of someone else is not dependent on their asking for it. You no longer allow unforgiveness to control your thinking and feeling.

Tristen's Buttermilk Pie Recipe

- 1 stick of softened butter
- 1 cup sugar
- 3 tbsp. flour
- 3 eggs, beaten
- 1 cup buttermilk
- 1 tsp vanilla *(Mexican Vanilla)

⚜ 1 (9 inch) unbaked pie shell

Cream butter and sugar. Add flour and eggs; beat well. Stir in buttermilk and vanilla. Pour into shell. Bake 45 to 50 minutes at 350 degrees. Cool completely before cutting.

End Points

Chapter 1 – I Thought He Walked on Water

[i] Lederer, William J. and Don. D. Jackson, The Mirages of Marriage, W.W. Norton & Company, 1990, pg. 42

Chapter 2 – Lonely Days and Lonely Nights

[ii] Craig Smith, Wives of Pastors Often Struggle with Loneliness, Stress, TRIBLIVE, September 6, 2009

[iii] Thom Ranier, Twelve Reasons Pastors' Wives are Lonely, Charisma Leader Magazine, 2/20/2014

[iv] Kahlil Gibran, The Prophet

[v] John Donne, No Man is an Island Poem, PoemHunter.com

[vi] LifeWay Research, Pastor Spouse Research Study, Survey of 722 American Pastor Spouses, 2017, pg. 51

[vii] Manhattan Mental Health Counseling, How to Let Go of the Expectations of Others

[viii] Walt Kelley, Pogo: We Have Met The Enemy and He Is Us, Published by Simon & Schuster, 1972

[ix] LifeWay Research, Pastor Spouse Research Study, Survey of 722 American Pastor Spouses, 2017, pg. 12

Chapter 4 – Sons of a Preacherman (PKs)

[x] Wikipedia defines PKs

[xi] George Barna, Prodigal Pastors' Kids: Fact or Fiction, 2013

Chapter 5 – Should I Stay or Should I Go

[xii] Shaunli Fledha, The Surprising Secrets of Highly Happy Marriages: The Little Things That Make a Big Difference, p. 178

Chapter 6 – Don't Be Cruel

[xiii] Church Leaders, by Brian Jones, How to Handle Critics, Complainers and Mean People, April 20, 2017

[xiv] Crosswalk.com, Thom S. Rainier, 7 Things Pastors' Wives Wish They Had Been Told, May 16, 2013

[xv] BrainyQuotes, Lewis B. Smedes Quotes

Chapter 7 – I Will Praise You In This Storm

[xvi] Michigan Medicine, Your Child Development & Behavior Resources, Children With Chronic Conditions, Nov. 2012

Chapter 8 – Graves Into Gardens

[xvii] Erica Borgstrom, A Look Inside Family Life When Someone is Dying, Discover Society – Articles, February 6, 2018

[xviii] Elizabeth Kubler-Ross, On Death and Dying, Scribner Publishing, June 9, 1997

[xix] David Kessler, Finding Meaning – The Sixth Stage of Grief, Simon & Schuster, Scribner, September, 2020

Chapter 9 – I Hope You Dance

Chapter 10 – We've Only Just Begun

[xx] Adam Folsom, What The Church Never Told Me About Dating, Nevertolddating.com, May 26,2020, Page 1

[xxi] Fable of The Four Seasons of a Tree – author unknown